From A CRY To A SHOUT!

Enough to cry, enough to shout

// From A
CRY

// To A
SHOUT!

Enough to cry, enough to shout

Pastor Robert Hendricks

Copyright © 2006 by Pastor Robert Hendricks

All rights reserved. No part of this book may be used or reproduced in any manner whatsoever without written permission of the author.

Unless otherwise indicated, scripture quotations used in this book are from King James Version, © 1999 by Thomas Nelson, Inc.

Printed in the United States of America.

ISBN 10: 1-59571-143-0
ISBN 13: 978-1-59571-143-4

Library of Congress Control Number: 2006929357

Cover Design — Damien Smith Photography

Word Association Publishers
205 Fifth Avenue
Tarentum, Pennsylvania 15084
www.wordassociation.com
1-800-827-7903

From A CRY To A SHOUT!

Enough to Cry
Less than ordinary
Son of an alcoholic
Molestation
Pornography
Health challenges
Parental blunders

Enough to Shout
Victorious consequences
Circumstances
God's providence
Deliverance
Spiritual emancipation

In my true life account, names have been changed because we are instructed, above all things have fervent charity among yourselves: for love shall cover the multitude of sins. — 1 Peter 4:8.

Special Gratitude

To my wife, Colleen Hendricks, and my sons, Adam and Tyler, who gave me space to grow.

With all my Love.

The Grasping For Life

Isaac prayed to the Lord on behalf of his wife, because she was barren. The Lord answered his prayer, and his wife Rebekah became pregnant. The babies jostled each other within her, and she said, "Why is this happening to Me?" So she went to inquire of the Lord. The Lord said to her, "Two nations are in your womb, and two peoples from within you will be separated; one people will be stronger than the other, and the older will serve the younger.

> *When the time came for her to give birth, there were twin boys in her womb. The first to come out was red, and his whole body was like a hairy garment; so they named him Esau. After this, his brother came out with his hand grasping Esau's heel; so he was named Jacob. – Genesis 25:21-26 (NIV)*

I certainly can appreciate and identify with the Biblical chronicle of Jacob. I was the ninth child of thirteen (nine girls and four boys) birthed from the womb of my mother, Velma Mae Hendricks. I am Robert Lee Hendricks, born December 7, 1956. During my identity years, I asked my mother to share with me my baby pictures, but there were none. To be honest, I have always felt a little different from my other siblings; for years I thought I was adopted.

My mother informed me that when I was born, I came out clutching my right hand like a fist—I still have the marks in my hand as a reminder. Marks are good for something, as the clutching of my hand at birth and the markings to follow were precursors to a tension-filled childhood which would ever impact my adult life, like two nations jostling. The jostle of a cry and a shout would be separated.

I was reared in the city of Compton, California, from grade school until high school. In spite of having twelve siblings, I did not realize God had landed me in a poor family until my young adult life. My father was an amazingly determined man, having initially less than a grade school education. He advanced his education after attending trade school, which landed him a job in construction as a plasterer. My dad was a very hard worker in this scrappy industry. I recall taking his work clothes to a neighborhood laundromat often to keep from destroying our already dated washing machine with plaster particles. My father would purposely leave a small amount of coins in his pockets. "If you find any money in my pockets, you can keep it." What a brilliant strategy, as my siblings and I fought to do the chore. Every once in a while, my dad mistakenly left more money than he planned. Of course I always returned it (okay, most of the time). My mother never worked outside the home other than taking in ironing from neighbors and friends of the family for a little extra spending money that she mostly spent on us. Mother never got her driver's license, and like my dad received little formal education. She was a dedicated housewife who inwardly held very strong Godly convictions bleeding out of her everyday life. Often she gathered us for Bible study, which she did her best to teach—mispronouncing words, if not falling asleep. To wake her up we would say, "Momma, the devil got you." She would say, "What, what, what, what." What a great laugh.

After a hard week of plastering, my father and his working buddies would go have a drink on Fridays to celebrate the end of a work week. This was non-problematic for my dad's buddies, but it was a missed hurdle for my dad as his drinking would continue through the weekends. This brought much tension, cursing, and fighting, mostly my mother receiving the blunt end of the madness.

Here We Go Again

It was not uncommon to have the police at our home, following my father's alcoholic rages and the fights he initiated with my mother. No one could out-curse my father; I mean he could put some words together that were very hurtful, yet hysterical. Sometimes I would find myself in a corner laughing so hard at his "colorful metaphors." I remember one evening my father, heavily under the influence of alcohol, decided that he was going to clean one of his shotguns (he had several). Not aware that the gun was loaded, he discharged the gun, creating several holes in the living room ceiling. The holes remained visible for months, a reminder of his drunkenness. If that was not crazy enough, one night my father came home fired up in alcohol, entering the kitchen with fire in his eyes as if mad at the world. He violently threw over the stove, breaking the gas line. You could hear and smell the gas escaping. Thank God that there was only fire in my dad's eye. The fire department came out to cap off the gas line. Once again, God protected our family, and Dad did no jail time for either events, but there was a hole in my heart, a burning cry inside desperately trying to understand why my dad would put those he supposedly loved in such danger.

My dad's love for us did radiate out, during the aftermath of another alcohol scuffle. I had walked home from George Washington elementary school for lunch. As I turned on to my neighborhood block, I could see from a distance what appeared to be a police car in front of our house. My heart began pounding as I thought, "What happened this time?" As I got closer to the house, I saw my mom talking to the police officer, holding her neck as blood trickled down. I would learn that my father had struck her with a garden tool. As I began to cry, my mom said, "Don't cry Robert, I am okay." With tears in my eyes, I looked to find my dad sitting handcuffed in the back seat of the police car. The police officer had left the window down where my dad was sitting, and my dad would say several times, "Officer, officer, officer, can I give my wife some money so that she can get food for the kids?" The moment my dad said that, my heart took another turn, a turn from anger to confused compassion. His words seemed to be saying he was sorry the incident ever got that far. His comments seemed to be saying, I love and care for my family. The police officer looked to my mom for her approval and then went and got money out of my dad's pocket. There I was standing, trying to balance the events during my elementary school lunch break. There were bittersweet reflections. I felt the love of my dad that afternoon, but he was going to jail. The bleeding from my mother's neck stopped and thank God she didn't require hospitalization. Before day's end my father would be released from jail, sober and apologetic. The events of this day were stored in my heart and mind as Mom and Dad seemed to get back to normalcy in their relationship. What was certain was that every explosive event was taking a toll on me, making me more nervous, more fearful, waiting for the next drunken scuffle from my father.

Why did God put me in this family? Why did Mom choose this man to be her husband? Why couldn't we all just run away from the madness? These were all questions stored in my mind, but they were too deep for me as a child to find answers. It seemed Mom's strong Christian values made her a sponge for abuse.

When Life Became Complicated

The 1960s rolled around; it was a time that I enjoyed playing marbles and G-I Joe with my friends. It was also a complicated time, the decade of Martin Luther King, Jr.'s speech "I Have A Dream," followed by his and President Kennedy's assassinations, the Vietnam War, and the first man on the moon. It would be a period of wonder and fear. I remember the Watts riot of 1965, the red-orange skies, the heavy smell of smoke from nearby buildings and businesses set on fire by angry protesters. It would be the first time that I would see real live army men (National Guardsmen) driving in my neighborhood. I had problems sleeping, wondering when the madness would stop. It would not stop until 34 people lost their lives, about 1000 were injured, and an estimated $200 million of property was destroyed. It would be the decade that brought us the Black Panthers, black militants practicing self-defense, and minority communities opposing the U.S. government. The Panthers fought to establish revolutionary socialism through large-scale organizing and community-based programs. All too complicated for a little ghetto boy. There was a Black Panthers' house on Stockwell Street not many blocks from our house in Compton. Life's casualties would even hit closer to home in 1966 when, as a ten-year-old, my family and I would get the shock of our lives. My father's alcohol abuse continued to rage, leading to more tension and scuffles with my mother. My oldest brother, Artis, would often come to the defense of my mother, literally getting in fights with my dad. Artis also had a close bond with my dad, since my father taught him the trade of plastering. This landed him a job with my father, while at the same time giving him financial independence. My father seemed to be proud that his oldest son was following in his work footsteps. This did not keep him and my dad from getting into altercations while dad was under the influence. These physical altercations were sad and frightening to me. Artis had gotten to the point that he could go blow to blow with my father, as my family and I looked on. At times I was proud that he stood up for my mother, and at times I felt he was out of place fighting with his father. But one evening all of that ended when we received the dreadful news that Artis, traveling from work to home, was involved in a fatal motorcycle accident. We never finalized how the accident occurred, whether he was forced off the freeway or lost control. What we would learn was that Artis was wearing his helmet, but it was not securely fastened. He hit a freeway guard rail and died later in a hospital, due to extensive head injuries.

His funeral service was held on August 6, 1966 at 10 o'clock in the morning. That morning, getting dressed for the funeral service, I noticed the house was very quiet. We all contemplated what we were about to experience. It would be the first time that I would see my father getting dressed in a suit and traveling to church with the family. What a time to do that. Transportation to the church would be a challenge. Although we had a station wagon, my father and my mother transported my brothers, sisters, and a number of relatives attending from out of state.

One of our neighbors offered me a ride to the service with him; it was just as well as I did not want my other family members to see me cry even before getting to the church. The tears began to flow the moment I opened my neighbor's car door, as he tried to comfort me. On our arrival at the church, we would see the hearse pull onto the property of Little Zion

Baptist Church. It was hard for me to understand and accept that Artis Gene Hendricks was inside. Although I did not wish for any of my family to die, I thought if God was going to allow for death, why not my father, who was the drunkard, the curser? My big brother was not supposed to die before my mother and father. There were no grief counselors back then; a kid in a large family was left to feel but not verbalize his feelings. So I hid them, and I was getting better at it every day.

Just like that, my big brother was gone. No more rides on the back of his motorcycle, going so fast that I could not yell, "slow down!" No more sips of his Welch's grape juice with Planter's peanuts added, no more smell of his new 501 Levis. No more walking in his oversized work boots.

My mother seemingly did amazingly well with the grieving process, but my dad was visibly shaken by my brother's death.

I suspected he had feelings of hurt and guilt surrounding the conflicts he had with Artis during his drunken episodes. Even my father's drinking subsided somewhat following the death of my brother.

All Because of A Sweater

My father loved the outdoors. Fishing and hunting were his great pleasures. He would often travel to Mexicali, the capital of Baja, California. This place, irrigated by the waters of the Colorado River, was great for fishing. Sometimes Dad fished strictly for pleasure and sometimes for commercial reasons; that is, selling some of his bounty to neighbors and others he met. Sometimes I would travel there with him and his "fishing buddies" as he liked to call them. It was one of the few events I enjoyed with my father. Traveling to Mexicali with my father following my brother's death was even more enjoyable, as my dad was much more placid, did not drink as much, and did little cursing. Boy, was it nice to leave the city of Compton for a place of dirt roads and dark nights with picture-perfect star-filled skies. It was so breathtaking to see falling stars. It was a place free of city noise. I was eager for nightfall so I could help build the campfire. And I loved the smell of smoke that lingered in our clothes. Lifestyle in Mexicali was much more primitive than ours. Families lived in adobe (a mixture of mud and dried straw) shell dwellings where cooking was done on open fire pits. It was the place that brought me the most enjoyment, the place where my father taught me how to set up my fishing rod and reel. He aided the process by cursing me out a few times until I got it right. Mexicali was the place where I learned how to cast out and how to reel in. I remember the day I caught my first fish. My dad had stepped out of my sight for a moment when there was a pull on my line, sending fright all over me. I began to scream, "Dad, Dad, hurry, I think I got a fish on my line!"

My dad came running, thinking I was in harm's way. He grabbed my fishing rod and reeled in the fish for me.

What felt like "Jaws" to me turned out to be a medium size blue-gill. I would eventually get better at reeling my fish in; the fight of the catfish was my greatest challenge.

The population in Mexicali was very poor, so much so that although we were from the ghetto, I felt rich in comparison. I remember one of my father's "fishing buddies" seeing children running up to the camper we were traveling in, asking for money. He took a handful of coins from his pocket and threw them in the street. His action was followed by mouthing off, "Look at those boogers run!" Despite being so young, I thought the action and comments of father's friend were insulting. I guess he felt important that day—what a jerk!

This same fishing buddy who tossed money in the street owned the camper we traveled in to Mexicali. My father shared the expenses of the trip. I recall colorful exchanges he and my father would have over who paid for the last gas fill up. The disagreement never seemed long-lasting, but it was a motivating factor of my dad wanting to purchase a small mobile trailer and boat. Then he would not need to depend on "Mr. Camper man" for traveling.

My father was very thrifty and never believed in buying on credit, although he pronounced it, "credkit." My father in fact was able before long to purchase both the mobile trailer and boat.

My father, who spoke very broken Spanish, met a middle-age man who lived in Mexicali and owned property. His name was Ramón. He was bilingual, which made for easy communication. My dad was able to negotiate a financial arrangement with him, leaving the mobile trailer and boat on his property and eliminating the need to transport the equipment each time we traveled from Compton to Mexicali. There were other campers that were allowed to use his property as well, and they became casual friends with my father. Ramón seemed to be a nice enough guy, making us feel comfortable. Many times he would sit around the campfire with us.

From 1965 to 1967, I must have traveled to Mexicali with my father at least six times. During one of these trips, some of my sisters and one of my older brothers traveled with us. It was during the time I almost lost my life. How? Well, my father decided that although we were under age, he would allow us to do some target practice, using a twenty-two rifle. We set up some cans on the ground and had a contest to see who could shoot down the most cans. My dad, supervising, opened the car door and rolled down the window so that we could use the car door for resting the barrel of the rifle, allowing more steady shooting. It was my brother's turn to shoot, and just when he was about to pull the trigger, I wanted to get a better angle of his shooting; instead of walking around the back of the car, I ran in front of the car door and barrel of the rifle. Without a doubt God spared my life that day. My dad yelled, "hold it, hold it." The curse out followed, but that day I was glad to hear any words from my dad as opposed to being dead. Needless to say, no more target practice, ever!

In 1967, I was eleven years old, and very small in stature for my age. Construction work was sometimes slow for Dad, which at times necessitated him to travel to Mexicali with the hopes of catching enough fish to bring back home to sell and make ends meet until returning to work. During one of these occasions, my dad asked if I wanted to go fishing. I happily responded yes, as it was during a school break. He and I would pack our clothes along with our fishing tackle and leave for Mexicali before dawn. My dad would say, "We are going to leave for day in the morning." What he meant was, before day. Like on Christmas Eve, sleeping was difficult because of the mounting excitement of leaving for Mexicali. As we turned onto the main dirt road leading up to the camp site, we were met by Ramón, who greeted us with a friendly welcome. We unloaded the station wagon that we drove in and surveyed and opened up the mobile trailer for lodging.

Mexicali—back again to the peaceful outdoor environment as I anticipated fishing with my rod and reel, along with campfires during evenings.

The first day was a time of setting out troutlines with the aim of catching a lot of fish in a small amount of time.

The next day my dad and I would get up early to do some rod and reel fishing about 10 minutes away from the campsite. The fishing was especially good, so much so that we continued at that site most of the day. When it hit dusk, the temperature began to drop. I informed my dad that I would be walking back to the campsite to grab a sweater before returning to catch the big one.

As I walked back to the campsite on the dirt road, darkness began to take shape. My ears were first met with the sounds of a barking dog, and to my surprise it was Ramón and his German shepherd walking towards me. Immediate fright and eeriness crept over me as Ramón and his barking dog got closer to me.

There was a cunningness that permeated out of the eyes of Ramón as he knelt down placing both of his sweaty clammy hands on my cheeks, whispering "nice." In his whisper I could smell his foul breath giving out the scent of alcohol. His hand would travel down to the crotch of my pants as he began to fondle my private parts, while trying to unzip my pants. I resisted, backing away and saying, "No Ramón, No Ramón." His dog barked louder, masking my plea for him to stop. He firmly placed his hands on my shoulders. Young and small, I was no match for him and his dog, as he maneuvered me into his adobe living quarters. It would be there that my senses were stunned by the smell of smoke billowing from his fire pit used for cooking, the smell of his sweaty foul body odor which he tried to disguise with cheap cologne. He sexually molested me with his dog barking all during the process. I could do nothing but comply, fearing his dog would bite me at anytime.

Once Ramón got his cheap thrill, which took just a few moments but seemed an eternity to me, he allowed me to walk away. His dog still barking, I left guarding my steps, walking backwards until I made it out of his adobe dwelling. With a sickening pounding in my head, once out of the sight of my perpetrator, I rushed to our trailer.

With all my strength I tried to wash his scent off my body, but the scent would become a fixture of memory, triggering flashbacks for too many years of my life.

What started out to be a simple ten-minute walk to retrieve my sweater would be a secret scar in my life for the next twenty-six years. As I ran past Ramón's adobe hut back to the fishing site into the presence of my father, I would not, could not, tell my father the awful thing which occurred to me ten minutes away from his grasp. Yes, my father who came running to my aid when I caught my first fish could not rescue me from the slimy hands of Ramón. Enduring a terrible headache, I behaved in the presence of my father as if nothing had happened. Why could I not tell my dad?

First, I blamed myself, thinking it was my fault—I should not have gone to get the sweater. Tell my father? He would have killed Ramón, and we would have never made it out of Mexicali. Tell my father? If I did that, I would never return to Mexicali, the place where I had the best time with my daddy. The place which brought me the most pleasure suddenly became the place which brought me the most pain.

My dad and I would not leave for home until two more days following the molestation. This meant that I would see Ramón a few more times, and I was very careful not to get too close to him. In the presence of my father, he would make eye contact with me; I quickly looked away with rage on my face.

I was so very confused as to how Ramón could be so

relaxed in the presence of my father after what he did to me. How did he know I had not told my father, or that I would not tell my father?

The two remaining days in Mexicali gave me more than enough time to question why Ramon would choose me to molest, how long had he been scoping me out unaware? I began to question events I observed during previous fishing trips to Mexicali with my father. My father and other campers, along with Ramón, during most fishing trips traveled together to what they identified as "going to town." I was never allowed to make these excursions. Some of the campers would return to the campsite drunk, while my father would return sober, although he seemed very happy.

I recalled one evening, after the men returned from "town," they all gathered around the campfire with laughter in the air. One camper pulled out a book of matches and invited me to open it. I opened the book of matches to find one of the matches designed into the form of a boy's penis, as they all laughed including my dad and Ramón. Even I gave a few chuckles. I thought about the time a group of campers returned from "town" with a young Mexican lady they had brought back to the campsite. My father had not made the trip with them this time. I was in our trailer relaxing and my father was stirring around the camp site when they arrived. I heard one of the campers call out to my dad, "Willie, don't you want to get in on this?" He would further make my father aware that one of the campers was having his way with this young lady as they spoke. I assumed she was a prostitute. By now I was hearing the chatter very well, and young Mr. Inquisitive decided he would look out the window to see what all the fuss was about.

Just as I peeped out of the window of the trailer, this young lady emerged in the camper door topless, baring her breasts. To the best of my knowledge, my father did not participate, but he was certainly hanging around with the wrong company.

My sweet mom, his wife, miles away at home, certainly would not approve of my exposure to that environment.

I recalled on other occasions Ramón's grandson and a retarded young man swimming nude in the river. At the time I thought it was the normal means of bathing, given the population's poverty lifestyle and no running water. All of theses events blended together following my sexual exploitation.

My final consideration as to why Ramón could feel at ease after molesting me was my memory of a Mexicali police officer who frequented Ramon's residence. He was huge in size, very intimidating, and a friend of Ramón's. Maybe his relationship gave Ramon a sense of security. Was this police officer somehow involved in some of the inappropriateness? All of these factors reduced me to wanting to get out of Mexicali with no desire to return. We would finally leave for home, but the damage was done.

The Shout!

Drunkenness is not only condemned, but highlighted as fulfilling one's uncontrolled desires... *Do you not know that the wicked will not inherit the Kingdom of God...nor thieves nor the greedy nor drunkards nor slanderers nor swindlers will inherit the Kingdom of God.*
– 1 Corinthians 6: 9 (a), 10 (NIV)

Drunkenness presents an admonition to believers...
Let us behave decently, as in the daytime, not in orgies and in drunkenness...Rather, clothe yourselves with the Lord Jesus Christ, and do not think about how to gratify the desires of the sinful nature. – Romans 13:13(a), 14 (NIV)

Alcoholism is a large health problem in the United States today, contributing to our moral crisis. This mood-altering drug plagued my dad's life for many years, negatively controlling his inhibitions and moral standards.

I feel so blessed that in my lifetime I was able to see my dad freed from alcoholism by the power of God and the support of Alcoholics Anonymous (AA). I am most elated that my father accepted Christ as his personal Savior receiving His forgiveness. Could I forgive my dad of his life's flaws? Without a doubt I could, and I did. That which stood high above his flaws was a father who ensured that his family never went without food or a place to live; a father who knew and taught his family the value of money; a father who never missed a day of work because of illness, or just because he was too tired to go; a father who sometimes worked seven days a week, including selling the fish he caught on fishing trips; a father who exemplified a strong work ethic, encouraging his children to do the same. The Spirit left my dad's body on May 12, 2001. I was privileged to give his eulogy.

The Book of Exodus speaks of an oppressive overseer or *taskmasters* who forced Hebrew slaves to complete public work projects for Pharaoh.

When I rolled *"taskmaster"* around in my mind, I equated the term with my sexual molestation, a taskmaster for many years.

> *And it came to pass in the process of time, the king of Egypt died: and the children of Israel sighed by reason of bondage and they cried, and their cry came unto God by reason of bondage.*
> – Exodus 2:23

> *And the Lord said, I have surely seen the affliction of my people which are in Egypt, and have heard their cry by reason of their taskmaster; for their sorrows...*
> *And I am come down to deliver them out of the hand of the Egyptians and to bring them up out of the land unto a good land and large, unto a land flowing with milk and honey...*
> – Exodus 3:7-8

I was never evaluated and counseled by a child and adolescent psychiatrist or mental health professional for my sexual abuse. Be clear, I am not saying that seeing a psychologist is wrong as an effort to deal with emotional and sexual trauma, I am simply saying that for me, God would use alternative spiritual interventions to free me from my "funk." I was crying, and my Creator was on his way to deliver me, transferring me to a place of well being.

For those of you who are dealing with Alcoholism or are in the family of an alcoholic, contact:

Alcoholics Victorious (503) 245-9629

Al-Anon & Alateen (818) 760-7122

For those victimized by sexual assault, contact:

The National Sexual Assault Hotline *1-800-656-HOPE.*

RAINN recommends the following if sexually assaulted:
- Find a safe environment—anywhere away from the

attacker. Ask a friend to stay with you for moral support.
- Preserve evidence of the attack—don't bathe or brush your teeth. Write down all the details you can recall about the attack and attacker.
- Get medical attention. Even with no physical injuries, it is important to determine the risk of STDs and Pregnancy.
- To preserve forensic evidence, ask the hospital to conduct an exam.
- If you suspect you may have been drugged, ask that a urine sample be collected. The sample will need to be analyzed later in a forensic lab.
- Report the rape to law enforcement authorities. A counselor can provide information that you will need in order to understand the process.

Remember it wasn't your fault.

Recognize the healing from rape takes time. Give yourself the time needed.

Know that it's never too late to call. Even if the attack happened years ago, the National Sexual Assault Hotline can still help. Many victims do not realize they need help until months or years later.

Plastered, Choked, Dying

Now in the sixth grade, I returned non-eagerly to George Washington elementary school with my molestation secret. My self-image was already damaged because of being held back in the first grade. My small stature lent a hand to my predicament, but I knew all too well that I was older than my classmates. The traumatic event which unfolded in Mexicali only made me more reserved in my social interactions, never allowing adult males to get too close to me physically or emotionally. My sixth grade teacher thought I was the perfect student. That year, my parents would attend open house and my teacher informed my parents, "Robert is the perfect student; he is so quiet in class." I cried inside, "But I don't want to be quiet." I desperately wanted to be like my other classmates who were social and held normal conversations. My perpetrator certainly knew how to screw up a kid's life. I looked forward to leaving elementary school that year to focus on junior high school. If only I could leave my baggage and pain behind.

In 1970, I entered Ralph J. Bunche, Jr. High School, "The Bulldogs." The school's football field was nicknamed "Gopher Stadium," as the field was riddled with holes from gophers. During football games players would sometimes suddenly go down, not because they were tackled, but because they stepped in a gopher hole.

Going through the adolescent stage is marked by the onset of puberty (for boys, it usually begins between the ages of twelve and fourteen). This period of my sexual maturation, as for most males, was a hormonal roller coaster fueled by all kinds of chemical messages.

I noticed dramatic changes taking place in my body such as hair on my legs, arms, and pubic area, along with the increased size of my sexual organ. Entering junior high school, I would be undressing for the first time in front of my classmates for Physical Education. Initially this was very difficult, but it also became beneficial as I made comparisons of my sexual organ with other boys. I said to myself, "not much difference there." I had initial suspicions about my male physical education teachers, because they were adult males. Fortunately no teacher or coach made any inappropriate advances towards me. My comfort level was even greater when other boys were there during my gymnasium interactions.

During this period of my life, my relationship with my father emotionally and socially was distant at best, but he did give me the nickname "Rabbit" because I was fast on my feet. The emotional pain of my molestation was somewhat deadened as I learned that I had a natural athletic ability given by God. I would use the ability by becoming involved in my junior high school track team. My specialties were the 100-yard dash and anchoring the four-forty relay. I often was victorious in both events. I started feeling pretty good about myself as coaches and classmates glorified my athletic abilities.

This all came to a halt the day I walked into the kitchen with no shirt on. I can almost today hear my mother saying, "Robert, what's wrong with your back?" Following a trip to our family doctor and a referral to a specialist, I was diagnosed with scoliosis (curve of the spine). Just like that, my life would get even more complicated. What the diagnosis of scoliosis meant for me was spinal surgery and a body cast.

What is a body cast? Think of a sleeveless T-shirt—everywhere this T-shirt fits on the body, I had plaster, yes from my waist up, hard plaster that made me feel hot all over. The body cast is designed for best healing following the surgery. The design of the cast gave me the appearance of having a hunch back. No longer was I the once glorified athlete; I was now the "Hunchback of Notre Dame," where my junior high school classmates found me as the springboard for poking fun and laughter. I recall one classmate having a bully type personality, telling a friend, "go ahead man, hit him in his stomach, hit him in his back, he won't feel it." As his friend followed through with his invitation, the punches just bounced off, causing no pain.

I would wear this body cast for over a year. Wearing it during the summer months was particularly challenging for me, as I was a very clean person. Okay, an overly clean person. Prior to the surgery and body cast placement, I took two to three baths a day. My need for multiple baths was the lingering effects of feeling always dirty after the molestation. Wearing the body cast presented a "sticky situation" for me as I could not get the cast wet; therefore, I was required to only take sponge baths. This caused a great psychological issue for me, as I thought I smelled (even if I didn't).

Sleeping was like sleeping on a rock. I tossed and turned, to my right, to my left, on my back, on my stomach. It was horrible, like sleeping on a rock; my stomach ached, and my side felt pinched by the cast. Needless to say, I did not get a lot of sleep—sometimes less than two or three hours.

At this stage of my life, there was a cry, a silent cry— *sexually injured, emotionally injured, self-image injured, I was a ball of frustration.*

One particular holiday, my mother and sisters were cooking a meal. I could hear the laughter coming from the kitchen. It seemed like they were having such a good time. Not me, I did not want to be a part of their little party. No, I wanted to isolate myself. Once the good smelling food was ready, I got my little plate of food and went to what my family called "downstairs" (only three steps from the kitchen). Feeling sorry for myself, I wanted nobody staring at me; on this day I would simply be in my own little world. I began to eat the tasty food; suddenly a piece of food went down the wrong pipe. Robert, who was eating alone, choked alone.

Gagging sounds followed as I desperately tried to get my breath. I began to sweat; I could not talk or cry for help. When I thought about the predicament I was in, plastered in with the body cast, I began to panic even more. I managed to muster enough energy to get to the kitchen where my family noticed I was choking. It all happened so fast. On the faces of my family read panic. I recall so well my mother crying out, "Oh Lord he is choking, what must we do?" My mother being very light skinned, turned red. I can still see the veins in my mother's neck being pronounced, which evidenced her concern.

My mother and sisters wanted to help, but did not know how to help; even if they knew how to administer the heimlich maneuver (which they did not), how would they administer it with this massive body cast I was wearing?

I felt myself losing consciousness, I felt myself dying. For a moment I thought it would be easier to die than to live. Have you ever felt that way? *My plan was just to die!* As I was fading away, all I could do is call on Jesus, *"Help me Jesus, Jesus, Jesus...Help me Jesus!"*

I found myself bent over at the kitchen sink, pushing my family away, that's what you do when you are in a state of panic, those who you love, who are trying to help, you push them away. But after I called on Jesus, the food was dislodged, and slowly I began to breathe again—sweat running down my face, *But He let me live!*

The Shout!

That day, I thought I was going to die. I did not have time to go to a prayer meeting, ask for my name to be placed on a prayer list. All I could do is *choke out, "Help me Jesus!"*

It has given me a new appreciation for *Jeremiah 29:11-13:*

> *For I know the thoughts that I think toward you, saith the Lord, thoughts of peace, and not of evil, to give you an expected end.*
>
> *Then shall ye call upon me, and ye shall go and pray unto me, and I will hearken unto you.*

Yes, that day I thought that I was going to leave this world, thought it was easier to check out than live.

I am so glad that the good Lord had some other thoughts towards me, and death was not His thought that day. He had thoughts of *"peace, not evil."* You see, *in my despair He was there.*

It was as if He was saying, "Robert, you don't think there is a future for you, *But I do.* Robert, I've got plans for you, you must keep living for I am going to get you out of this body cast. You've got to get saved, one day you will be married, you will have kids. Robert, that evil that someone perpetrated on you, someday you will be able to talk about it, preach about it and help millions, yes Robert, *You have a future!"*

Just like the scripture says in *Jeremiah 29: 12, 13,* that day I called upon the Lord, my mother called upon Him, my sister called upon Him. We prayed and He listened. I sought Him with all the fading life I had, and *He helped me. I am so glad my help came from the Lord!*

Just before starting high school, I did get out of the body cast. When it came off, I felt so light; the dust and smell vanished. I have come to know Jesus delivers you, saves you:

He lifts the burdens off you, he cleans you up!

Mary, the mother of Jesus, and Jesus and his disciples had all been invited to a wedding. Jesus' first miracle took place at this wedding reception in Cana of Galilee, turning water into wine.

It was a good thing that Jesus attended this wedding as the groom's family was in a sticky situation. They were expected to provide all the refreshments for the festivity. To run out of wine would be a disgrace and not hospitable. It was the very situation this family found itself in. The solution to the problem was to involve Jesus, and that is just what Mary did. She went to her son, Jesus. Mary reported back to the hosts of the wedding, here is the deal, "whatever he says to you, do it." Yes, Jesus came to the rescue, producing wine in abundance.

The folks at the wedding in Cana had more wine than they ever needed. The wine was poured, and all the people present rejoiced at the rich abundance. They had never tasted such fine wine before; in fact, the headwaiter wondered why the good wine had been kept back. In most cases the best wine came first, the wine not having a kick came later, when folks heavily under the influence could not tell the difference. – *John 2:1-11*.

In the Jewish culture of that time, wine symbolized joy. Rabbis had a saying, "without wine there is no joy."

It was a wonderful evening for my wife Colleen and I to have been attending a wedding in beautiful Long Beach, California, in November 2005. The wedding was held in a historical church dating back to 1866. The edifice was spectacular, including a 70-rank Moeller organ with 4,226 pipes, reportedly being one of the finest pipe organs in southern California. Once the wedding started, many in the audience were mesmerized by the entry of actor Jamie Foxx (childhood friend of groom) as a groomsman and singer in the wedding. The reception was held at the famous ocean front

Reef restaurant. As my honey and I sat at our assigned table, we had an opportunity to reflect on the wonderful evening we were taking in. What would be the most remembered? The beauty of the historical church? The beautiful wedding including a surprise participation of actor Jamie Foxx? No, it would be what God arranged at the reception.

We had no idea that we would be sitting at the table with a man who had played NFL football for a short period of time prior to some misfortunes. This man and I attended the same church as children. He was 7 years my junior. He knew me during the time I had my bout with scoliosis, requiring me to wear the body cast. So here we are, nearly forty years later, he begins to share with Colleen and me, with so much passion, how I enthralled him. "Robert, my brother and I looked up to you, how you carried yourself. My brother and I would go home imitating you, practice being like you, we wanted to be just like you. Even when you came to church in your body cast, we looked up to you. Robert, I loved how you carried yourself." Imagine, words never spoken to me until this night. At that time I was feeling so icky from the sexual abuse, and guarded due to a poor self-image. Now to know two young men were studying me without my knowledge. To know that I impacted their lives in a rich way that evening brought great joy.

I am so glad that Jesus showed up at the wedding to remind me that He is still pouring out rich wine. He is still the giver of abundant joy.

For you who carry physical limitations, who have emotional scars, who have faced ridicule, don't give up on life! Trust God; one day you will get a release from Him!

The Pornography Revenge

It has been said that being a sexually victimized male is likely to lead you into a lifestyle of homosexuality.

Let me be clear here: although I did not embrace homosexuality, there was sexual inappropriateness that occurred in my life following the sexual molestation.

My education about sexuality would not and did not come from my father, period, end of story.

I laugh at my mother even today, as I think about her advice on sex. She said, "You better wait until you get married before you start having sex. I know a man in my home town who messed with girls before he was married, and he had to carry his sacks (testicles) in a wheel barrow."

If mom only knew someone had already messed with me sexually and had messed up my young head. This internal conflict made my quest for answers sexually and socially revolutionary.

The revolution started at my home mailbox, progressing to adult bookstores and theaters. Sometimes the revolution was pleasurable, exciting, confusing, scary, embarrassing, miserable, and most of all destructive. All fueled with an attitude of revenge toward my sexual predator.

You can say the progression started in innocent fashion with magazines from department stores like Sears, Zody's, and J.C. Penney's. As I flipped through the pages I would travel from the appliance section to the sporting goods. Curious Robert found himself in the women's underwear section, peeping at panties, bras, and more.

Before long I was skipping all the other sections. I traveled straight to the women's underwear section, delighting my eyes, feasting and imagining. I began to find the so-called, "soft core" pornography—which pictured sexual acts that were not illegal in magazines such as Playboy, Penthouse, and Hustler. As far as I am concerned, all were knocking on the door of hard core pornography. Where did I find these displays of pornographic material? I found them in neighbors' garages, on neighborhood streets, in grocery and liquor stores, and in poorly discarded trash. I would borrow the magazines; let me be honest, I would steal them. These adult magazines became my "rush," using my internal feelings of shame and filth. Because of the evil that was done to me, I felt it appropriate to engage in immorality, and I was ripe and eager to return evil for evil.

My pornography tools came by accident but would lead to deliberate acts. I would hide them in my clothes, under boxes in our house, under mattresses, inside box springs, inside pillow cases, inside trash cans, under trash cans in the yard, and in between pages of my school books (parents survey all these areas). I felt so adult-like looking at the materials, not reading much, but looking much, flipping the pages, over and over again, using the treasured material as tools for arousal and masturbation. Did I say that? Yes, that's what I said.

As odd as this might sound to some, because of my scarred thinking at that time of life, pornography became a tool of revenge, a counter for being sexually molested. My innocence was stolen by a man when I was a helpless boy, but now I am in control, yes, in control of pornography, so I thought. My introduction to adult videos came at the expense of my father cleaning out the apartment of a relative who died at an old age.

This relative had been active in his church. My father brought some of his boxed belongings to our home. One day while looking in one of the boxes, I found a small film projector with several reels of film. After setting up the projector for viewing, I hit the "on" button switch, and I can still hear the clicking sound in my mind today as the film made its way through the projector. Appearing on the wall of the room in which I hid myself behind a locked door, was the most perverted black and white hard core pornography that I had yet seen, including "group sex." Following the viewing, I said to myself, "Okay this is wrong, and I should not be doing this. I am through with pornography, I am going to stop." I put the projector along with the film back in the box, and stored it in what our family called "the little house" (a small storage room that my father had built). Well, I did stop for 2-3 months, but the pornographic nightmare started again as those illicit sexual images crept back into my fertile mind.

So Proud To Be A Rabbit

In 1973, I would leave the Compton School District and start my high school education at Long Beach Polytechnic High School. The school mascot was a rabbit. Interesting to me because my father had given me the nickname "Rabbit."

My high school proved to be a cultural awakening. Previously living and going to school in the city of Compton provided mostly interactions with Blacks and a few Hispanics.

This was not the case at Long Beach Poly, as it provided an environment that was well diversified racially, making for great interracial interactions. I still recall the exciting football games at the Long Beach Veteran Stadium (all these years later, I still peep at the newspaper to see how the "Rabbits" are doing in football), eating pizza at Me & Ed's pizza parlor, and the hype of arriving on campus at 5:30 a.m. to set up for the Annual International Fair held there.

Not only did I bring to Long Beach Poly good grades (which continued throughout the three years), I brought my sexual molestation, which was now in the seventh year of secrecy. I was still having my scrimmages with porn. I had accepted that I was no longer in control of it; it was overpowering me just like my sexual perpetrator had done to me at age eleven.

My appetite grew more and more for those images as they seemed fastened to my being. You might say I could smell locations of pornography. I recall getting a clean-up boy job at an apartment complex.

My job responsibilities included washing down the sidewalks surrounding the complex, cleaning up the laundry room, and emptying all the small trash cans into a large trash dumpster that was on the back side of the apartment complex. One day, as I was emptying some trash into the dumpster, I had to step up on some type of wooden crate to see over the top of the dumpster. Prior to emptying the trash, I looked in, and there in plain view, my eyes met a hard core pornographic magazine, which led me to jump into the dumpster to feast my eyes. I got into the trash to look at trash.

Why Did She Let Me In?

When I was sixteen years old, I made a "PPM." What is a "PPM?" Premeditated porn move (I coined), another form of my revenge. Yes, I would set out to get into a XXX movie under the age requirement. I took my student picture ID card and birth certificate. Anyone looking at my date of birth should have determined that I was well under age to enter an adult movie theater.

I jumped on the bus and traveled to Long Beach where I had spotted this XXX adult theater located on Ocean Street. I walked towards the ticket booth, casually looking over my shoulder to see if there was anyone who might recognize me. There was no one in sight. As I approached the ticket booth, I came looking like a kid, about 130 pounds, just slightly over 5 feet tall. As I got closer to the booth, there, flowing in my spirit, was an almost cocky confidence. I thought to myself, she better let me in knowing what I have gone through in my life (how would she know?). When I finally reached the ticket booth, this middle-aged woman glanced at me with sort of a smile, she told me the price of the ticket, never questioning my age, never asking me to show ID.

But why did she let me in? Was it to set me up for further sexual exploitation? Was it an opportunity for someone to abduct me like thousands of other children? Was it making another buck to add to the billions of dollars made in the porn industry? As I walked toward the entrance of the theater, there were butterflies in my stomach. I entered the theater, which was very dark and smoky from the foul smell of cigarettes, and almost stumbled into my seat.

Waiting for the movie to start, I began to relax and feel like, "I was the man." I took out of my front pocket a crumpled up cigarette I had stolen from my dad. I lit the cigarette and began to smoke and choke. For that moment, I felt so adult and in control. In my warped way of thinking, this experience was like a trophy of revenge, yeah, right! When the XXX adult movie finally hit the screen, the vile deeds and sexual acts in very graphic color, quickly brought arousal mixed with nausea and nervousness. I could not stay in my seat. I managed to find my way to the restroom, and once inside I was alone standing at the urinal when I heard the door open and a man entered. There was an incredible wave of fear that came over me when this man entered the bathroom and stood in front of the urinal next to me as I began having sudden flashbacks of what happened to me in Mexicali in 1967. I finished relieving myself and rushed out of the adult theater. Once outside the theater and walking towards the bus stop, how relieved I felt as I evaluated the risk I took on this "premeditated porn move." I began to see how my sexual molestation was at the hand of someone else, but this sexual roller coaster I was now on was at my own hand. This need for revenge became self-destructive as I became a slave to lust. And this lust was always growing and never satisfied. Feeling empty and sorry for myself, I had to return to the dark secret to begin to lift myself out of this sexual funk. It was at this juncture that there was a glimmer of fighting back as I realized the act of my molestation was over, but my perpetrator was still winning as I chose to get revenge in such a sick and compromising way. It merely added pain to injury. One thing for certain, I was good at keeping secrets; the problem was I was hiding very serious secrets which were crippling my adolescence.

My quietness, often mistaken for good behavior, only confounded the problem. As I continued high school I would have a lot of victories not falling to the temptation of pornography, but I would also have some slips, which would bring about major letdowns at the end of the day.

I Let *Jesus* In

I met several friends and was doing well scholastically, but the hurt was still deep. I tried to mask the hurt by putting forward highly superficial social fronts. My friends thought I was so happy and together, but I would go home so empty and broken.

I recall one Friday going home to my room in so much emotional pain, tired of the fronts, having been brought up in the church; I acknowledged that I was a sinner *(Romans 3:23)*, knowing that I needed God and not wanting to be distant from Him *(Romans 6:23)*, accepting that Jesus died for me that I could experience life, eternal life, too *(John 3:16)*, and that Jesus was ready and willing to come into my life *(Revelation 3:20)*. That night I asked Jesus to come into my life, and boy did He!

You can ask Christ to come into your life also, even prior to completing this book. If you have not done so, do it now.

E-mail me (www.newtestamentchurchla.org) so that I can rejoice with you and help you grow!

I began to grow spiritually, becoming a member of the

Agape Christian Club, at Long Beach Poly. I started attending and then joined Great Hope Church of Christ Holiness in Long Beach. I would visit other churches of my classmates, and started going to Christian concerts, my first one being Andréa Crouch at Melodyland in Anaheim (I took the bus alone). I went to places like Calvary Chapel in Costa Mesa with Pastor Chuck Smith. I remember the good Christian Fellowship and what we call the "afterglows" at Bob's Big Boy and Norm's restaurants. I recall the hunger for God's word, often going to Christian bookstores like the Lord's and Lighthouse Christian bookstores. I enjoyed listening to Christian radio, to such programs as: *Focus on The Family,* with Dr. James Dobson and *Grace to You,* with Pastor John MacArthur, Jr. Listening to Dr. Vernon McGee with his southern voice was also one of my favorites.

Christian music artists also helped me to grow spiritually, as I would rush to pick up the latest albums from artists like: Honey Tree- *Clean Before My Lord* and *Resist the Devil;* Andrea Crouch & the Disciples- *This is Another Day, Perfect Peace, We Expect You,* and *If Heaven Was Never Promised to Me;* Keith Green- *No Compromise, Make My Life a Prayer,* and *To Obey is Better Than Sacrifice;* The Way- *New Song* and *You Are Caught in the World-Caught in the Crowd;* Maranatha 5- *Falling;* Love Song- *Love Song, Freedom,* and *Feel the Love.*

These artists and songs spoke to where I had been, where I wanted to go in life, and what I wanted to be in life. I was not there yet with my struggles, but God had begun a good work!

After becoming a Christian, I would learn that Don, a classmate, was also a Christian. Don was into reptiles. He someday wanted to become a veterinarian. He had a very large pet snake he kept in a cage in his home. I was not fond of snakes, but tolerated Don taking me to his house to see this large monster. Don, this curly haired Irish young man, sometimes obnoxious and loud, took an interest in my spirituality. It was he that taught me the importance of having devotionals and journaling. Yes, Don was quite a character. I remember having lunch with him at a pizzeria on 7th Street in Long Beach. When he had to take a restroom break, a customer in the next booth said to me, "How do you put up with that guy? He talks so loud!" When Don returned, I just smiled never telling him the comments the customer made. That was Don; he played in our high school band, and in my opinion was not very athletic—I mean he did not have the skills I did. One Saturday morning, Mr. Don challenged me to a game of tennis. Although this was not my best sport, "no problem, I can beat non-athletic Don." Well, Don ran me all over the tennis court, putting a good beating on me.

Don, a Christian longer than I, became my best friend, but I could never tell him what happened to me as a child. Being a Christian made me more relational, even to the point that I got up enough confidence to ask a Christian young lady out to our senior prom. It was "puppy love" infatuation, but she turned me down. This was a blow to my confidence and ego. My heart broken, I never pursued asking anyone else to the prom. Don had a pretty Christian sister he introduced me to. She had beautiful reddish-brown, waist-length hair. Her hair truly was her glory. Too bad I did not have enough courage to ask her to the prom, but we did become an item prior to graduating. I remain loyal to Long Beach Poly High, the home of the "Jackrabbits." I graduated in 1976, the bicentennial year, with honors and scholarships. I graduated with a great spiritual awakening, but still having told no one of my sexual molestation occurring ten years earlier.

The Worth of Hurt

How proud I was to start college at California State University, Long Beach following summer break after high school graduation.

Initially being overwhelmed by the size of the campus, with over 33,000 students, the inability to find my classes, and failing several exams, I eventually settled down to feel more comfortable being a "college student."

The relationship that had started at the end of my high school year at Long Beach Poly with Sue continued. She and her family lived a few blocks away from the modest apartment I rented not far from the campus. I was able to rent this apartment using some of my college scholarship funds. Sue was in love with me, and I thought I was in love with her. This was my first serious relationship. Sue made my weekends and holidays special. I looked forward to spending time with her. Our relationship had its built-in challenges that some interracial relationships experience. When alone, we felt so comfortable being together, but when we were in public, I could feel people staring at us as we held hands. When I brought Sue home to meet my family for the first time and to attend a family picnic, my family made no obvious difference accepting Sue, but in my heart I felt there was reservation on their part. I had multiple interactions with her family, including going to their church and eating dinner in their home. Her father, an artist, even painted a portrait of me.

Sue never voiced any reservation about our interracial

relationship. But this was a sometimes on, sometimes off relationship. Why? Because I had on-and-off struggles in my head—especially about relationships.

I got into the relationship to prove that I could be in a physical relationship and there was no doubt that I got into the relationship because I was hungry for love, real love. Sue brought out the best in me. But worse was in me too, and she had no clue. I was double dating her; she was not competing with another real life young lady, but with vile sexual images from porn that began to peak again. Can you imagine that? I was once again obsessed into this vicious cycle. I still knew where most of the adult bookstores were in Long Beach. Boy did I envy the persons working in these bookstores saying to myself, "It must be nice having their job, you can look at pornography any time you want." There were a lot of occasions where I would go to the movies alone. I had searched out the movie section of the newspaper, looking for R-rated movies only, as this rating would give me the best opportunity to see nudity without going to a XXX adult theater to which I had vowed never to return. Forget about the plot of the movie, I wanted to see nudity. Some movies would carry an "R" rating not because of nudity but because of violence, or strong language. Sometimes I ended up in violence only movies. Boy! Was I mad to have spent money with the anticipation of feasting my eyes on nudity but seeing none.

When I would see nudity it was never enough, because I had already seen so much more in my young life. It had consumed so much of my thoughts, I went to bed with it on my mind, and I awakened with it on my mind.

Sometimes I wanted to see it more than I wanted to eat a meal. With porn I could pull it out when I needed; other than the expense, it was so much easier to manage. Who needed a physical relationship? I was having a visual relationship with an individual I would never see in real life or meet personally, yet I was feasting my eyes on these images. On some occasions, I would see young ladies walking on city streets who did not know me from Adam. Some dressed provocatively and others did not. I would find a way to undress them in my mind, fantasizing what I could do with them. Talk about warped thinking. I would go into liquor stores convincing myself I was there to buy a soda and newspaper, when the real reason I was there was to peep the porn magazines. Often I bought all three items to make myself feel less guilty. I entered conventional bookstores and used bookstores, knowing that they would have adult book sections, where I would find myself after a quick look over my shoulder to make sure no one I might know was looking. There was so much inner turmoil going on that I would emotionally distance myself from Sue. I would tell her that we needed to slow down the relationship, hiding behind the interracial challenges excuse that I partially created in my mind. Knowing the real reason for the distance, I was feeling guilty because I enjoyed porn more than I enjoyed her.

What struck me on one occasion of viewing porn was the young look of some of the ladies I was viewing. I began to question, "how many of them were doing what they were doing by choice, or were they lured into a compromising position?" "How many were under age?" "How many of them were raped?" I thought about my nine sisters and how I would feel if they were on the other side of the camera, doing what these young ladies were doing. More guilt and more pain.

Sue was such an innocent and yet spiritually mature young lady, while I was less spiritually mature and brought a lot of unresolved baggage into the relationship.

I thank God, knowing it was His grace that we never had premarital sex, because I certainly had enough sexual images from porn in my head that could have steered me there.

There would be one final episode that would permanently end our dating relationship. It would be the result of what I call "a Spiritual identity roller coaster." Here I am clamping down on the close of my first year in college, when I became intrigued by the thought of becoming a missionary in the Philippines. Why a missionary? Why at that time? I could say, it just had a special ring to it and I was motivated by an older sister who had received some missionary training. It is safe to say that both of these reasons factored in.

As I have processed the event, it was an additional opportunity for me to try feeling spiritually better about myself, an opportunity to further run from my past.

The passion, the ring of "Robert Hendricks, missionary to the Philippines," more and more captivated my thoughts and being. When I shared my desires with Sue, she projected mild excitement, wrapped in confusion. "How would this affect our relationship?" "Would there be a relationship?" All good questions I was unwilling to answer at that time. What was certain, I was on a mission, a mission to be the "great Missionary."

Since I was on my way to be that "great missionary," I needed a missionary training school, not California State University Long Beach. Never mind that I would be losing my full scholarship there (scholarship prohibited any gaps in my educational attendance). With that, I made arrangements to leave college and enrolled in a small nine-month missionary training school in North Long Beach, the very school my sister once attended.

As I reviewed the school curriculum and enrollment policy, I came to know that I was required to live on campus, with a strict policy embracing no co-ed dorms and no co-ed swimming. Oh yes, there was one more nugget tucked into the school admission requirement. Unless you entered the school married, no dating was allowed. I had to swallow hard on this one. What? Was I entering a cult? No, just a strict accelerated missionary training school which would be requiring me to give up my apartment, and a way out of an up-and-down relationship with Sue.

It was a beautiful southern California day as Sue and I sat on the grass at Heartwell Park.

I had brought her there to break the less-than-beautiful news that we needed to end our relationship to allow me to concentrate on missionary training.

Sue sat quietly, head down, brushing her nails together. She finally looked up with tears in her eyes. She communicated that "she thought this would happen." I was crying inside that I had hurt a beautiful young Christian lady, and there was just so much she did not know about me.

Crying inside because she thought I was this strong young man who held strong Christian values. If I could just tell her that I was still running from my childhood molestation. Yes, I was crying inside over trying to run away from the shackles of pornography, which unknown to her placed a wedge in our relationship.

What a day. It was a long walk back to the car, as we walked from the park, no longer hand-in-hand, but side-by-side.

There was not much conversation as I drove Sue back to her home. I must say, driving away from her home, there was the feeling of a ton of bricks being lifted off my shoulders. Not in the sense that I was glad to get rid of Sue, but knowing Sue deserved better, not to be hurt by a young man of unresolved hurt and secrecy. The end of this relationship would be a landmark in my life, not to return to being a slave to pornography. It would take confession, repentance, and a lot more in my spiritual journey.

I started the missionary training school with excitement and the eagerness of obtaining great spiritual insight. Insight that I felt would advance me to the mission field, in addition to handling my secret life conflicts. Well, God had other plans, He would honor my obedience of leaving Cal State Long Beach for missionary training, but I would soon learn a lot more about myself.

I first learned that there was a lot that I did not know about the Bible and that I had great fear of sharing my Faith.

The Missionary Training School was big on "door to door witnessing," and the school provided many opportunities to do just that.

I recall being teamed-up with a training partner, who approached a door with such ease it seemed. He would spill out, "Hi, my name is Mike, and this is Robert, we are Christians in your neighborhood; we were wondering if you have a Bible in your home…?" As long as Mike did the talking and I did the praying, it was cool. When it came time for me to "take a door," I froze, heart beating fast, and stumbling for words. It was very unnatural for me.

I remember my partner and I going to a very wealthy neighborhood in Long Beach called Bixby Knolls. As we approached the large, luxurious homes with expensive cars in the driveways, I thought to myself, "How can I tell these people Jesus can make a difference in their lives, when they had so much already." My partner would remind me that, "they had souls, and they needed to have the opportunity to get to know Jesus, too."

I got more comfortable doing "door to door witnessing," but it never felt natural for me.

Witnessing, emphasized so much at the missionary training school, became a big bondage for me.

I thought I had to share Christ with everyone I came into contact with…at the bank, at the bus stop, at the grocery store. When I failed to do so, I felt so bad, so convicted, so guilty.

Now at the missionary training school for almost eight months, there was a little over one month to go prior to deputation and then being sent to the mission field. As was the case during pivotal times, I was having serious reservations and doubts about continuing.

I questioned why the missionary training school waited until the eighth month of training to request students to seek reaffirmation of God's missionary calling, through a special time of prayer and meditation. Following this sacred period, we would be reporting back to the school board with the results. As it turned out, the timing was ripe for me as I in fact had been having second thoughts as to why I was there, and what the future held for me.

Those days of deep soul searching with the Lord proved to be gut wrenching but very revealing. I came to realize and accept I was at the missionary training school on my own doing, and not His calling.

I was there to become more spiritual, and becoming more spiritual was supposed to take away the pain of child molestation and the scars of pornography, which I was thankful I had not returned to since the break up with Sue and entering the missionary training.

Yes, I was there to improve my self-esteem; people would look up to me. I could hear them, "Look at this spiritual giant who sacrificed so much." What a foolish thing to do. What a waste of time.

Missionary Drowned, Cal State Re-found

Not really, because God would honor my misguided obedience. He would use the experience to thrust me eventually into a ministry of another sort.

As I went back to my missionary counselor to inform him that God had released me from the missionary training school, it was less than acceptable to him. He would schedule time for me with the "higher ups" of the school. The majority of them said I was making a big mistake. "If you leave this school, Robert, you will be out of the will of God, your future would be filled with regrets and unhappiness."

What they did not know was that their tactics to keep me there made it easier for me to leave.

I had already been injured enough in my life and certainly did not need their guilt-persuading tactics to keep me there.

I packed my little rags and left! I decided I would return to Cal State Long Beach, although minus scholarship, and minus the relationship with Sue, who was now attending UCLA pursuing her nursing education.

I returned to my parents' home in Compton for a short period of time while reapplying to and waiting for my acceptance of enrollment at Cal State Long Beach. I would finally receive the acceptance letter, "O Happy Day!" I would be majoring in social work with a minor in marketing.

I would be returning to Cal State Long Beach a full-time student. No scholarship, but with grants and near full-time employment at a Carl's Jr. Restaurant, it was doable.

Housing could have presented a problem, but God's providence gave me a sweet arrangement.

I had stayed in contact over the years with my junior high school Spanish teacher and sponsor of the Knight's Service Club (for honor students). I had been the president of the honor club. Mr. Wright was a bachelor living in San Pedro, California. He had previously taught in Japan for many years. Japan made such an impact on his life that he designed his home Japanese style to include a Japanese sand garden, a Japanese hot tub, and sun deck.

His home overlooked the Long Beach Harbor and the exclusive Palos Verdes Estates.

Mr. Wright, who likes to be called "W," offered me free housing minus food responsibilities to help me resume my education. It made for a very nice, quiet environment conducive to studying. I will be forever grateful to "W" for taking an interest in a ghetto boy he taught in Compton.

The Shout!

Back in 1976 when I asked Christ to come into my life, there were no doubts. He came into my life despite the bouts I continued to have with pornography into my early college years. Eternal life was a reality, and through God's empowerment I would grow spiritually mature.

When I was consumed with pornography, a little was good and more was better!

I remember trying to heal myself of my porn addiction by making deals with God. I said, "Lord I am going to slowly detoxify myself; I will watch a little porn every once in a while, and then I will lose interest." This treatment plan always led to more. My second plan was to have a binge on pornography. Getting the vilest XXX adult videos, magazines, books, and peep—all of them in one setting. After I finished viewing to my delight, I said to God, "Okay that's it Lord, I got enough, no more." This was another lie, because it always led to more viewing, even following long intervals of not viewing. Oh, the frustration and anxiety I felt, letting God down and questioning if I would ever be able to give up pornography completely. I started believing God's Word, hanging my hat on,

These things I have written to you who believe in the name of the Son of God, that you may know that you have eternal life, and that you continue to believe in the name of the Son of God. – 1 John 5:13

Being confident of this very thing, that He who has begun a good work in you will complete it until the day of Jesus Christ. – Philippians 1:6

Confession

Thank God for *confession*. I accepted and confessed that I was powerless over porn, that it had the best of me. No longer was it a weapon to deal with my childhood sexual abuse. It was an addiction, and it was consuming my spirituality and my time. It was keeping me from being relational, other than with sexual images. I felt so nasty about how much nasty I allowed in my life.

As I look back over my life, God in His awesome providence knew during the early stages of my Christian life I would have difficulty allowing men to get close to me emotionally, given my childhood baggage; therefore, he used a classmate (Don) in high school, Ministers of the Gospel on the airwaves, and Christian Ministers of Music to speak truth into my being for discipleship purposes.

I came to know the importance of God's Word, letting God clean my house—all that vile stuff. I finally began to embrace His Word for a great solution.

> *Your Word I have hidden in my heart that I might not sin against You. – Psalm 119:11*

God allowed me to hear, learn, and embed His Word into my life.

It was essential that I take advantage of what I had inside of me, "the mind of Christ." I began using His mind and not my sick mind!

> *For who has known the mind of the Lord that he may instruct Him? But we have the mind of Christ. – 1 Corinthians 2:16*

I liken my previous pornography-driven life to a glass. A glass that was first empty, but then become dusty. Becoming dusty on the outside with all kinds of sexual subliminal (acting on our subconscious) messages. These messages, very subtle and faint from billboards, and TV commercials, but all impacting the cleanliness of the glass.

I began to take directly inappropriate sexual images (dirt) into my system (glass). Pouring in pornographic magazines, videos, etc. This glass, no longer empty and clear, but clouded. When I was consuming pornography, I was emotionally spent—hiding stuff, watching over my shoulder, hoping that no one would find me out, see me in the wrong bookstore, purchasing the wrong magazines. I was feeling increasingly guilty over the vile stuff I was viewing and reading. All the inappropriate language and vileness which came with it. It was destroying me spiritually.

Thank God for reminding me of a man named Lot who captured the pages of the Bible.

> *It would be possible to be delivered from an environment of oppression, the conduct of the wicked.— Genesis 19:9; 2 Peter 2:7-8*

If my mind was going to be clean and clear, I would need to get more of God's Word inside of my glass, I would need to become fully irrigated with His Word.

Thank God for the river of life; it reminds me of a little song my college friends and I would sing, *Spring Up O Well.*

"I've got a river of life flowing out of me, makes the lame to walk and the blind to see, opens prison doors, sets those captive free, I've got a river of life flowing out of me. Spring up, O well within my soul, spring up O well and make me whole, spring up O well and give to me that life abundantly."

As I continued to allow the *Living Water of God's Word* to flow inside of me, overflowing, cleaning the inside and the outside, as I embraced more and more of God's Truth, I was set free! God's word allowed me to maintain freedom as I embedded it in my heart, as I made application of it in my life. I'm really talking about the *Spirit-Filled Life. What is that?* Allowing the *Holy Spirit* to guide me into the truth.

> *...And it is the Spirit who bears witness because the Spirit is Truth. – 1 John 5:6*

As I submitted to the Spirit-Filled Life, those vile images

were being replaced with the power of the truth. It captured and changed my lifestyle. I was no longer guided by some porn star or model.

> ...He, the spirit of Truth, has come; He will guide you into all truth... – John 16:13

When I was using porn, better yet, when porn was using me, it was being hid in the secret chambers of my heart/mind, as I allowed it to take residence there.

I shout because the Spirit-Filled Life motivated and empowered me to allow God the Father and God the Son to take full residence, serving porn an eviction notice.

> Jesus answered (speaking to Judas) and said to him, if anyone loves Me, he will keep my word; and my Father will love him, and We will come to him and make Our home with him. – John 14:23

> The Holy Scripture says, If we confess our sins, he is faithful and just to forgive us our sins and to cleanse us from all unrighteousness. – 1 John 1:9

> Yes, I breathe out confession to receive the cleansing of sin. – Romans 10:13

> I confessed with my mouth the Lord Jesus Christ and believed in my heart... – Romans 10:9

Dear friend, I can shout Victory today, but what I had to learn of my inappropriate sexual desires outside of marriage was not sitting well with my Creator. There were lessons to be learned from Leviticus 18 and 20:

Sexual intercourse was equivalent to *uncovering the nakedness* of a person. *The man who lies with his father's wife has uncovered his father's nakedness; both of them shall surely be put to death (dealing with incest).*

When I was viewing pornography, I was committing acts of immorality by uncovering a person's nakedness. This uncovering of nakedness was a sexual act which should only take place under the union of marriage.

Understand, God is not trying to take away the pleasure of sex. He wants us to get a "rush" from sex, but it should be enjoyed within the union of marriage, as spoken in the revelation of God's will.

> *Marriage is honorable among all, and the bed undefiled; but fornicator and adulterers God will Judge. – Hebrew 13:4*

When I was getting my thrill lusting over pornographic acts, I was not fulfilling God's will for my life.

> *You have heard that it was said to those of old, you shall not commit adultery. But I say to you that whoever looks at a woman to lust for her has already committed adultery with her in his heart. – Matthew 5:27-28*

Yes, back then without question, my looks and thoughts were over-involvement of lust, more than appreciating God's blessing women with beauty. There was the desire to be sexually involved. The lustful concentration came through the media of magazines, videos, women walking the streets, and even sitting in church. My mind and intent were way out of the boundary of purity.

The Truth of The Matter

Pornography is such an important topic as it unites or arouses our sexual desires.

An article from the *Christian Research Journal*, Volume 27, Nov. 3, 2004 reported the following:

"During the single month of January 2002, 27.5 million Internet users visited pornographic Web sites."

"Americans spent an estimated $220 million on pornographic Web sites in 2001," according to a New York-based internet research firm (in 2005, Americans were expected to spend $320 million on porn sites).

Battlecry.com reported, "teenagers are the first generation to grow up with point-and-click pornography. 90% of teenagers have viewed porn online…most while doing homework."

Battlecry.com further reported, "teenagers have seen nearly 14,000 sexual scenes and references each year on television. That's more than 38 a day."

Sit down on this one: the Colorado-based Focus on the Family organization reports that "7 out of 10 pastors who call their toll-free helpline claim to be addicted to porn."

My body is wonderfully made. My delivery would result from understanding that my body was the temple of God, that His spirit resides inside of me. Further, the Holy Scripture says, *"that if anyone defiles His temple, including myself, God would destroy him."* Why? *"Because the temple of God is holy,"* which temple I was. – 1 Cor. 3:16

I certainly did not want to commit suicide, being on the wrong side of God. I would learn to watch and pray; I am not talking about pornography.

Repentance

Following confession, I had to *completely* turn away from porn, complete separation from this bondage that had plagued my life. The porn toxicity had to be eradicated in a radical manner. I could not keep one magazine, one video, one cut-out centerfold picture, *I had to get rid of it all.* I could not go down certain streets where I knew adult book stores would be there waiting for me. I exchanged the vile master pornography for God.

Releasing and allowing the Spirit of God to run my life.
– 2 Chronicles 7:14

If I was going to remain walking in victory, I could not let my guard down; in other words, I needed to "watch and pray." It would be a matter of guarding my heart.

When I was consuming pornography, I was emotionally spent—hiding stuff, watching over my shoulder, hoping that no one would find me out, see me in the wrong bookstore purchasing the wrong magazine. *Thank God I am free!*

Words To The Wise

Let me say to you who have recently given up the life of pornography: You must do what you need to do to stay clear of entangling again, even if you do it by removing cable TV and staying away from movies and TV programming which project sexually charged behavior. You may need a filtering device for your computers. *You must separate and leave no forwarding address!*

Boundaries

Abstain from every form of evil. – 1 Thessalonians 5:22

There was a need for me to set a safe distance between myself and porn, that which had ensnared me, that which had crippled me in the past. I could not then and cannot now get close to the evilness of porn, feeling that I am strong enough to handle a little eye observation.

"Form" speaks of that which attracts the eyes—any form of what is evil (pornography would certainly fall into that category), is not acceptable to God, and therefore should not be practiced or viewed by believers (indulged). Listen, I don't care how spiritually mature you think you are, under the right temptation (perhaps I should say wrong), you are not beyond falling. *Believe that!*

Boundary setting was a must for me. I would be fooling myself if I thought I could come right up to the edge of the boundary and not be enticed. I had to construct a boundary around my boundary to maintain a safe distance. My deliverance from pornography was not to play games with pornography, a little or a binge, but total abstinence.

> *Put to death, therefore, whatever belongs to your earthly nature: sexual immorality, impurity, lust, evil desires...*
> *– Colossians 3:5.*

Accountability

Finally, I needed a few men who could help me to stay true to my transformation, to keep me on the right track.

> *And Saul also went home to Gib'-e-ah' and there went with him a band of men, whose heart God had touched.*
> *– 1 Samuel 10:26*

I needed, and God blessed me with spiritual men whose "...heart God had touched (that which was lacking earlier in my life)." Men who continue to help me walk in integrity, men whom I am accountable to, who allow for truth to be spoken with compassion. Men who are aware of my past, who know the stronghold porn had in my life.

Men whom I don't need to be surface with, men whom I have given permission to ask if I am maintaining my integrity.

A safe environment offers confidentiality, a place where they and I can share our genuine struggles, failures, and growth needs.

The Lord has presented many opportunities in different venues to share my story. Sometimes being so candid with my previous <u>s</u>ecret <u>s</u>exual <u>s</u>truggles (SSS, Woo!) will draw a reaction from "spiritual giants," who will quote to me the following scriptural text:

> *For it is shameful even to speak of those things which are done by them in secret.* – Ephesians 5:12 NIV

Timing is Everything

It is not my desire to offend anyone, rather to expose the danger and wear and tear of sinful behavior. *The habits of a transgressor are hard.* – Proverbs 13:15

A further reading of Ephesians 5 has the following teaching:

> *But everything exposed by the light becomes visible. For it is light that makes everything visible. This is why it is said: Wake up, O sleeper, rise from the dead, and Christ will shine on you. Be very careful then how you live not as unwise but wise. Making the most of every opportunity, because the days are evil.* – Ephesians 5:13-16 NIV

I shout because I speak from victory and not from enslavement. In exposing the dirtiness of porn, I speak from light and not from darkness. Exposing the dirtiness of darkness (porn). I share my once secret sinful behavior as a means of countering and rivaling the wrong behavior.

Songwriter, David Lloyd wrote,

If I Can Help Somebody

If I can help somebody as I pass along.
If I can cheer somebody with a word or a song.
If I can show somebody they're traveling wrong.
Then my living shall not be in vain.

If I can do my duty as a Christian ought.
If I can bring back beauty to world up wrought.
If I can spread love's message that the Master taught,
Then my living shall not be in vain.

Solomon, a student of wisdom, who had much understanding along with wealth, said:

> *To everything there is a time to every purpose under heaven... Time to weep, and a time to laugh, a time to mourn, and a time to dance...A time to love, and a time to hate, a time of war and a time of peace.* – Ecclesiastes 3:1, 4, 8

Timing is everything. I turned down a TV interview in Southern California, with a well-known author of five New York Times bestsellers, a doctor, and host of an internationally syndicated radio program. Why? Because timing is everything; simply, I did not have the peace of God.

The timing was right following a meeting with Pastor Ralph Martino. In 2004, Pastor Martino, a Web Cast host (VoiceAmerica.com), invited me to share my story of being sexually victimized, and being a slave to pornography (four hours of interviews) to an audience across the world. How I thank God for empowering me to be transparent, not for the sake of being transparent, but to be a freeing agent for many. Here are just some of the written responses I received following the interviews (some names have been changed for confidentiality purposes).

When A *Secret* Is Revealed

"I just finished listening to your web cast with Pastor Ralph. First, I want to commend you for being able to tell your story.

"Even though it took 27 years, you were still able to come forth and free yourself from a secret you had carried and burdened yourself with for all those years. Praise God for the release. Your interview was very touching to me, especially the part you spoke about not letting what happened to you control your sexuality.

"I have a dear friend that was sexually victimized by his

uncle. Unfortunately, this did affect his sexuality, and he is now gay. For him not to have had the experience of being with a woman always baffled me. If he takes you out, he is a perfect gentleman (open doors, pulls the chair back, puts arms around you, etc.) but yet still prefers men.

"Continue to share your story. My son was at the convention on Tuesday night when you preached, and when I went home on Wednesday, he asked me if that was the first time you had spoken about being molested. He was very interested in your story. At that time, I didn't know much about the circumstances, but I will be sure to let him listen to the interviews also.

"You are truly a man of God, and I thank Him for allowing you to have the courage and faith to set yourself *free*.

Keeping holding on to his word,"

Jackie

•••

"Thank you Pastor, for your openness and honesty. I know it took a lot to get to this point, but your testimony will be the key to open the hearts and minds of others that have gone through similar situations.

"I know a fraction of what you went through. My grandfather attempted to molest me when I was 12 years old. I think I was about 19 or 20 when I finally told my mother.

"He was her stepfather, but we all knew him to be our granddaddy. Growing up, all the kids were really close to him and extremely fond of him. He took us out on trips and to the park and stuff, and he had this pickup truck that all the kids like to ride in.

"I remember overhearing a conversation that my mother and grandmother were having, and my grandmother thought he was cheating on her. Shortly after that, I noticed his behavior changing toward her, but he still loved us and remained the same with us. Then one day, I was at his house with him and my aunt who was about 8 years older than me. He was going to take us out for lunch. He sent her around the corner to the store to buy some punch. I didn't understand why she needed to get punch when we were going out to lunch. Neither did she, but she went anyway. When she left the house and was out of the gate, he asked me for a hug and a kiss, which was not uncommon. He was a big jolly guy and everybody loved him and was appropriately affectionate with him.

"But this hug and kiss started out a whole lot differently than normal. I pulled away and asked him what he was doing. He asked me again for a hug and a kiss, and I refused and threatened to tell. He backed off and gave me money not to tell and said he was sorry and that he'd never do it again.

"When he died my mother was baffled as to why I wasn't going to the funeral. I told her. She believed me. I never told my grandmother or my siblings. The only other person I told was my husband.

"I'm still a bit uncomfortable talking about it, but as with other situations I've experienced, I'll use it as a testimony if it will help others to confront or deal with issues that are deeply hidden and shameful.

"I have been blessed and encouraged by your life and your testimony and pray that the Lord will continue to use you to open and illuminate our hearts and minds to realize that through *Him* we can be set free. GOD BLESS YOU!!"

Amble Thomas

• • •

"It has taken me quite some time to listen to it. The reason is I have struggled myself with pornography, and I have been delivered from it through Jesus Christ.

I would constantly find myself going to the video store and tempted to go to the adult section 2-3 times a week for the last

3 years. It took so much of my time and my soul, it hurt so much that I felt I wanted to die. I thank you for your testimony about this subject. I haven't gone to the video store for a while now, and it's only because I have stayed in the word and prayed to God and talked to others about it. There is so much more I could say but I just wanted to thank you and let you know that I struggle too."

Katie Myers

• • •

"Pastor Robert, I just finished listening to the interview and I am so completely proud of you and your courage and your testimony. I am sending the site information out to everyone that I know because someone will be healed by this interview. You were very eloquent and well-spoken and just plain awesome. Congratulations. I know God is using your testimony and I can't wait for the book!"

Toni

• • •

"I finally got a chance to listen to the interview…What a touching story! I know you are free now that you shared this valuable information. For 27 years you were hurt, but I am glad you did not give up and certainly God did not leave you. He had a plan for you. A story to tell. Now you can tell your story and His story.

Praise the Lord! Keep preaching, teaching, and proclaiming the Good News. For, Great is the Lord and Greatly to be praised. Be Blessed."

Larry

• • •

"Pastor Robert—I listened to the program tonight. Obviously, I never knew anything about your situation until tonight. It's very sad that these things happen, yet I'm sure God will use it and you to minister to help many who have suffered in the same way. I know that it took a lot of courage on your part too. Thanks for telling me about this. God bless."
John

● ● ●

Thank You Lord for teaching me through relationships!
I thank God for Don, who became my best friend in high school. I know now that Don was a special instrument God used to help develop me spiritually. Don administered discipleship to me, a new convert, without ever conveying it as being discipleship.

Thirty-two years later, Don's influence still spiritually enriches my life.

> *Go therefore and make disciples of all nations...teaching them to observe all things I have commanded you... – Matthew 28:19,20*

God revealed a lot to me following my first dating relationship with Sue (Don's sister), the young lady who came into my life at the end of my high school year.

It was not the interracial component that made our relationship wavy, but my messed up head.

> *And He has made from one blood every nation of men to dwell on all the face of the earth, and has determined their reappointed times, and the boundaries of their dwellings.– Acts 17:26*

Young ladies like Sue, who are spiritually grounded and spiritually protected, should be highly commended. Sometimes

God allows such young ladies to interact with young men who have sexual baggage and messed up heads, young men who are spiritually immature, who have difficulty expressing and receiving real love. I say to all the young ladies who have been hurt by young men like me, who knew no better, *We are sorry, and thanks for being Godly young ladies.* We can now say sorry, because through the power of God's Truth our minds have been renewed and transformed.

Bronze, Blonde and Freckled

As I settled back into California State University at Long Beach, I joined a college Christian club on campus called, *Christ Is the Answer (CIA)*. The club was founded by a spirit-filled, charismatic, and gifted young lady, Ingrid Mosley. Ingrid and I previously shared membership in the *Agape Christian Club* at Long Beach Polytechnic high school, where she was no less brilliant.

Christ Is the Answer met both on and off campus. Ingrid was a member of a prominent Black Baptist church in Long Beach called, *Christ Second Baptist*, where her grandfather, Herman Gore, was the Pastor. Ingrid, would invite members of her church to attend the off-campus Bible study and fellowship of CIA. We met in a spacious upstairs room of a Church in Long Beach on Thursday nights.

I will never forget the Thursday night when up the stairs walked a bronze-skinned, freckle-face, blonde knockout. She was wearing tight-fitting Levis with leg creases pre-sewn. She was an invited guest from Ingrid's church. We, a multi-ethnic group gathered in a circle, began to sing with a guitar, *Marantha* songs. When it came time for sharing prayer requests, the "knockout," being introduced as Colleen, opened her mouth, "Please pray for my family," she said. How could such a noble, sincere prayer request sound so profound, luscious, and sexy to me?

Was it because I was relationshipless? Or, was it just pure lust? God forgive me, but it was both; she was one fine "thang," one fine blessing from God who knocked me off my feet! What a beauty! Okay, I need to stop here; I am having a flashback! Colleen came to the off-campus Bible study and fellowship several more times with her girlfriend, making it hard for me to concentrate on the spiritual. I would sneak a glance at her every once in awhile, I think unknown to her. Her tender eyes, her freckled face, her nicely formed lips captivated my attention. I melted when she spoke; yes, I was in love with this woman to whom I had said very little. I thought, "the next fellowship I will get to know her more, maybe even ask her out, yeah, that's what I will do." The boy was "sprung"!

Call it fate or call it God's will. The next Thursday night, I was anxious to get to CIA's Bible study and fellowship. I was ready to get to know Ms. Colleen better. I had rehearsed what I was going to say to her, to get her to go out on a date. In enters Colleen with that normal cheerful face, but what's this, she is flanked by a male. Not just a male, it was Terry.

Terry and I had been high school classmates, in fact we were in the same club—*Distributive Education Clubs of America (DECA)*. He was the president, and I was the vice president. I had not known that Terry and Colleen were an "item," until Colleen introduced him as her boyfriend. Yes, here it is years later I find out he is dating the woman that I was infatuated with.

"Hey Terry, good to see you," I said as I tried to regain my composure, stepping back into the gentleman role, you know, the spiritual. I had to bounce back spiritually, slap myself in the face.

I chalked it up, accepting that Terry was one blessed brother! I was determined that God's timing would bring about the right relationship, if there was going to be one.

Colleen continued to come to the Thursday night Bible study and fellowship, sometimes with Terry and sometimes without Terry.

To my surprise, one Thursday night, Colleen came to the fellowship changed. That bubbly personality that I had come to expect was missing. That evening after the fellowship, she confided in me that her relationship with Terry had ended. Her question about lifestyle issues caused so much dissension in their relationship that he moved to Texas. I promise, I had nothing to do with it!

Could it be that God was opening a door for Colleen and me? A relationship to be born? A love story in the making? Not so fast, there was a fatal attraction waiting in the wings.

A minister who had known both Colleen and Ingrid had started attending the Thursday night CIA Bible study and fellowship. He had learned of Terry and Colleen's ended relationship. He managed to approach Colleen, informing her that God had given him a "revelation." Woo! Woo! The old "revelation" move. What was the revelation? The revelation was, "Colleen, God told me that you were going to be my wife." Yeah right, I thought.

For Colleen, I had become a spiritual counselor as she confided in me that she was shaken by his so-called "revelation." She was shaken by it as the minister was living out this "fatal attraction." He would show up at her home unannounced and at odd times. Colleen related a time when "she opened her front door to go to work, finding this minister standing outside her door."

She further communicated that she was afraid that it would get uglier and more dangerous, and she asked for my advice.

I said, "Colleen why don't we plan on getting together to have some tea to further discuss the situation and possible options." She agreed to a restaurant counseling session.

What?

Colleen and I would have our date, I mean our counseling session, at the Park Pantry Restaurant on Willow Street in Long Beach. As we sipped on our hot tea with lemon, I shared with her how the minister's "revelation" was so misguided and self-serving. I said, "If God had spoken to the minister as he said He had, God would have given her some kind of heads up." She said that was not the case, and that she just wanted him to leave her alone. I agreed to talk to "The Man of God" man to man and from a spiritual perspective, in other words, "get lost Bro!"

Okay, mission accomplished, counseling session over, we can go home now, right? Not yet!

I broke all of the counseling rules, but it felt so good being with Colleen. The lady that I had been so infatuated with is sitting in front of me seeking my spiritual guidance, that's right, me—the boy from Compton. Was this really happening? Should I pinch myself under the table to make sure I was not dreaming?

That night Colleen shared more about the circumstances of her ended relationship with Terry, and I shared about the circumstances that ended my relationship with Sue.

We were both ripe for a relationship with each other. Yes, the unthinkable occurred. We left the Park Pantry Restaurant that night, I having asked Colleen to pursue a relationship with me.

I had that spiritual talk with Mr. Minister; he got the message and sought for another "revelation."

Chicken, Cadillacs, I'm Gone!

Going back to my experience at missionary training school, that pivotal day when I sought reaffirmation from God as to whether I was to continue on the road of becoming the "great missionary," I mentioned, "God honored my misguided obedience and used the experience to thrust me eventually into a ministry of another sort."

Well, that day as the tears fell, as I poured out my heart to God, expressing my frustrations in regards to my life being one big pile of turmoil and miscalculation, God both comforted my heart and gave me a divine plan for my life, that I would run...run... run... from.

That day, God took me to the following scripture:

> *So I said: Woe is me, for I am undone! Because I am a man of unclean lips, And I dwell in the midst of a people of unclean lips; For my eyes have seen the King, The Lord of hosts.*
>
> *Then one of the seraphim flew to me, having in his hand a live coal which he had taken with tongs from the altar. And he touched my mouth with it, and said: 'Behold, this has touched your lips; your iniquity is taken away, And your sin purged.'*
>
> *Also I heard the voice of the Lord, saying: 'Whom shall I send, And who will go for Us?' Then I said, 'Here am I! Send me.'*
>
> *– Isaiah 6:5-8*

And just like that, in such a tender moment, God spoke to me through His Holy Scriptures. Like Isaiah, God reminded me that my life had been less than pure, that I had been broken down with so much drama in my life. But thank God for His sanitizing work, purging me and making me spiritually fit to become a mouth-piece for Him. That's right, that day God called me to be a "Preacher Man." *The Missionary Training* saga was part of what needed to happen on the way to fulfilling God's call on my life .

But, would I answer His call? Would I say, "Here am I! Send me"? Who me, a preacher? Not me, I'm out of here, gone!

You see, my script of how I felt about being a preacher had been written by my father's feelings about preachers, and what I had observed on a limited basis myself. An obvious stereotype, I thought what was most important to black preachers was "Driving Cadillacs and eating chicken." I did not want to have anything do with that, "so just find someone else Lord...Someone else Lord!" "Not only that Lord, what if I am making another mistake, just like I made losing my college scholarship to go on this missionary safari? No, No, I ain't doing it, Lord!"

Well, having that calling tucked away in my heart, one day on my way to Cal State University Long Beach, I was rear-ended on the freeway by a diesel truck. While my Mustang was totaled, I was shaken but uninjured. As I stood on that rain soaked freeway waiting for the tow truck, I was physically, as well as spiritually, jarred. "Thank You, Lord, for saving my life; I could have been dead," I expressed in my heart.

That day God reminded me of His calling on my life, and it was on that day that I said, *"You got my attention Lord, send me!"*

I preached my first Gospel message at a small church in Long Beach, called Greater Hope Church of Christ (Hol.) U.S.A. With my sweetheart Colleen in the audience along with my high school and college friends, I was so very excited and nervous. I don't remember what Gospel message I preached; in fact I hope I did bring a Gospel message.

Greater Hope Church took some getting used to as it was unlike my early Christian church experiences that had been mostly multi-cultural and non-denominational. The worship style was different, and the dress style was definitely different, "what was up with those hats the sisters were wearing, and the suits and ties?" I was accustomed to wearing my Levis or Cords (Corduroy), never suits and ties. I had attended churches where young ladies wore pants and shorts. Oh well, I got accustomed to it and gradually made changes in my attire. *Greater Hope Church* was a "family church" (many were related), and there seemed to be a spirit of mediocrity. Most Sundays services did not start on time, and messages were legalistic—many sermons about what you should or should not wear. I could go on but I won't, because there was love flowing there, coming from God's people, His creation. I was thankful that God gave me a place to belong.

The Shout!

And the Lord God said, "It is not good for Robert Hendricks to be alone, so give him a helper." Praise God that He formed a young beautiful lady whose name is Colleen Tidmore. God brought her to me, a young man who had been through so much in life, a young man who had been delivered from so much in life. A young lady who completed and complemented my life with her spiritual insight and support. with her spiritual insight and support. Yes, on that Saturday, August 1, 1981, at twelve noon, she became Mrs. Colleen Hendricks. Bone of my bones and flesh of my flesh. We became one flesh. Colleen, after almost twenty-five years, still does wonders for my well-being and continues to bring out the best in me.

Your past does not dictate your destiny. God always has a better future for us. God in His awesome providence was not only freeing me from the pain of molestation and delivered me from pornography, but also He blessed me with a wife who runs circles around, and is far better than, any touched-up artificial image. No longer is there a need for me to fantasize over adult magazines, videos, and the like. Mrs. Coco is my true love, romantic, fulfilling my needs with blissful satisfaction. I know this is mighty steamy, but "We's" married!" My friends say, "I smile a lot when I am with Colleen." Yes, I smile a lot because I know who is next to my side as I drink from my own cistern. Hey!

Marriage should be honored by all, and the marriage bed kept pure... – Hebrews 13:4

Drink water from your own cistern, running water from your own well. – Proverbs 5:15

If I Am In Class

My college life was now in full swing. I was beyond being envious of the "rich kids" who were being put through college by their rich parents, they were classmates who did not need to work—just study, eat, sleep, and attend classes. I was married, working, and juggling classes to try to finally finish up on a bachelor degree, a degree that would take five years to complete following my time away at the missionary training school. I was even more determined to complete my college education, as I would be only the second family member (first male) of thirteen to complete his education at a university level.

Finally, it came to my last semester at California State University at Long Beach. Colleen and I resided in a small modest apartment in the "Wrigley District" of Long Beach. Colleen and I were almost nine months pregnant; okay, she was mostly pregnant, and I just helped out a little.

Not wanting to stretch out my college life another semester, I acted as superman. While continuing my employment, I requested and was granted a petition to take 21 units (full time was 12 units).

Uncertain if I would be in class when it was time for Colleen to go to the hospital to deliver our child, I made pre-notification arrangements with the campus police. If by a slim chance, I would find myself in class at baby delivery time, Colleen (Coco) was to notify the campus police to get me out of class in order to meet her at the hospital, about ten minutes away from campus.

Colleen was to notify her mother, who lived nearby, to transport her to Saint Mary Medical Center, where she would be delivering our first child. I covered all the bases, never thinking we would actually need to activate the plan.

Waterfalls

March 2, 1983, was a windy and rainy night as I sat in my Social Work Community Policy class, populated mostly by females, which had been the case for most of my Social Work classes. I was immersed in the lecture given by the instructor, who happened to be a priest. In the middle of the lecture, a tap on the door and then in peeped a campus police officer with water dripping off his uniform hat. "Is there a Robert Hendricks here?" There was pandemonium in the classroom, as my classmates had been made aware of Colleen's pregnancy and the notification arrangements I had made with the campus police. I sat there in shock as he asked the second time, "Is there a Robert Hendricks?" "Yes, that's me," I managed to barely get out of my mouth, filled with so much emotion and shock. The officer, with a big smile on his face, followed by saying, "Get to the hospital!" Yes, Colleen's water had broken. Pandemonium broke out again among my classmates. I leaped up, leaving my rain jacket, not even asking the officer for a ride to my car. I ran in the rain to my car for my trip to the hospital. As I traveled, it was raining so hard, it was like being under a waterfall. A normal ten-minute drive took me five minutes. Okay, so I ran a few red lights (Sorry Lord), hydroplaned a few times, but I got there safely.

As I approached the hospital information desk drenched in water and drenched with nervousness I said, "Hi, my name is Robert Hendricks, my wife is having a baby, and I was to meet her here."

"Just a moment Sir," the information clerk (Nun) said. While she was on the phone checking, in walks Mrs. Colleen

If I Am In Class

grimacing in pain, her mother at her side. Yes, I had beaten Colleen and her mom to the hospital.

We were then assisted by medical staff to the maternity floor, where the pre-delivery journey began, and boy, was it a journey!

Now, I had gone through all the classes the hospital had offered to assist my precious to get through the labor pain—how to assist her with breathing, how to hold her hand, how to speak encouraging words, and the whole gamut. It wasn't working!

I sat at the bedside, holding Colleen's hand, and mouthing what I thought were comforting words to her. Delight to my ears, Colleen cried, *"Go get my mother!"*

Celebrating, I said to myself, "Thank You Jesus! Thank You Jesus!" I hurriedly summoned my mother-in-law and then collapsed onto the waiting room chair.

It was a long night, but on March 3, 1983, I was summoned by the medical staff to quickly get dressed into my scrubs. It was "show time," Colleen had already been taken to the delivery room, and baby was on his way! At my arrival in the delivery room, Adam Colbert Hendricks was on his way out. Dad had to watch while the doctor used forceps on his baby's head to position it for delivery.

It was a procedure that Colleen I questioned for many years, as our son was left scarred with head indentations from the forceps. We were young parents for the first time, and so happy that God had blessed us with a beautiful boy—seven pounds and one ounce, nineteen inches long. Because he was our first son, we named him Adam. Using parts of both of our first names, as he came from both of us, we gave him the middle name, Colbert. We were so proud and anxious to get Adam home, but Adam would not be coming home right away, as a medical crisis had developed.

Adam had developed jaundice—a medical disorder characterized by yellow discoloration of the skin and eyes (the result of the presence of coloring matter from the bile). Colleen would be released from the hospital a few days after delivery, but our precious first son would be staying behind in the hospital under a heat lamp (part of the treatment plan). It was so hard to leave our little one there that we both cried. Both Colleen and I questioned God's purpose in his allowance. Colleen even thought it perhaps had something to do with our naming our child Adam, that God was cursing us for choosing a name that had also brought a curse to mankind. Boy, were we twisted. What made the situation even more difficult, Colleen had started breast feeding Adam during her stay in the hospital. The doctor, feeling it best for her to continue, directed her to pump milk from her breasts at home. We traveled to the hospital every day, several times a day, to feed Adam with the breast milk that was placed in a bottle.

We were glad to see and hold him each visit, but it was so very hard to leave him, knowing that he would be placed back under the heat lamps until the jaundice had been cured. "Would he be cured?" "Would there be more complications?" These were all the thoughts that trickled through the fabric of my mind. I never consciously allowed myself to wrestle with Adam's survival. Our family brought much emotional care and support for us during that time.

Following six days of Adam's extended hospital stay (it seemed much longer), we finally received good news, Adam was well enough to come home. After a waterfall of events, Adam would be coming home the next day, but there would be one more waterfall to occur.

Beaming with excitement, I hooked up the baby car seat given as a gift and drove over to the hospital, smiling all the way. My baby is coming home! Colleen, family, and friends stayed back at the apartment, making preparations for our bundle of joy who would shortly be there.

I carefully strapped Adam in the car seat and made my way

towards home. Living in an apartment, our parking space was located in the back of the complex. Well, I was so excited about having Adam home and wanting to get him inside as fast as I could, while parking the car I got too close to the main water valve (it controlled all the water in the apartment complex). I hit it and water shot up in the air, like one giant waterfall.

What a way to cap off a week. And speaking of capping off, because I did the damage, I had the responsibility of calling a plumber to make the repairs. I was so embarrassed, as the whole apartment complex was without water until the repairs were complete. Once again, family and God's people rallied around us for support. One friend from Colleen's previous church was there preparing a meal for us when the mishap occurred; she was able to call her brother who was a plumber. He came right over and capped off the water and the drama for the evening.

Well, the rest is history, Adam made a full recovery from the jaundice, although if you look closely, I think he still has indentations on both sides of his head from the forceps used at the time of his birth. At this time of writing, Adam is twenty years old, living with a roommate in Compton, and working two jobs, both significant because as you recall I was born and raised in Compton. You will find out soon that there was a period of my life that I worked two jobs, so stick around!

What a wonderful and proud day for me when I did finally walk across the stage to receive my college bachelors degree in social work. It brought special meaning to me to have in the audience my sweetheart Colleen and my mother and father, who had not been to many of my special events while growing up due to his alcoholism. But here he was, in full sobriety for many years now, hearing his youngest son's name called for a college diploma.

Mr. Wright, "W," my former junior high school teacher who had provided free housing for me while attending college, was also there. Wow, what a special day. A reception was held in my honor. In attendance were many of those who had touched my heart over the years but who still did not know about the hurt that was done to me when I was eleven. That's right, other than my wife, I told no one else about my sexual molestation even at this adult stage of my life.

A Giant with a Limp

Now that college life was over and I was a parent for the first time, I settled into ministry, you know, being a "Preacher Man." I made sure not to eat a lot of chicken, and no way was I driving a Cadillac. But I did meet a special man, a pastor who drove an outdated brown Cadillac. He was a man standing tall in charisma and inspiration. He would become my mentor.

It was one Saturday morning, Deacon James Calhoum and I were conversing in the parking lot waiting for the start of our district church convention when a brown dated Cadillac drives into the parking lot. Out of the Cadillac comes a distinguished looking man with smile on his face. He walked with a limp (childhood injury), carrying a newspaper under one arm and a Bible under the other. His name was Pastor Ron Crammer, Jr. (later to become Dr.). I had heard about this Pastor, "as being on the cutting edge," pastoring a church called New Mount Church, in Los Angeles." A church known for "very lively services," in the mind of some, "a very liberal church." Most agreed, "Boy, the church had a powerful choir"—if the choir was singing at any event, folks wanted to be there!

That day I officially met Pastor Ron Crammer, Jr. As our eyes met in the parking lot, he stopped to talk with me. No wonder he was a giant in the eyes of others (shedding tears as I write this), he took time to find out who I was.

It seemed like he had known me for a while, a very down-to-earth man, who had already impacted the lives of many and started to do the same for me. From that day on, a very special relationship was in the mix.

The relationship with Pastor Ron Crammer would continue to blossom, as both Colleen and I got to know his wife Betty and him a lot better. They took a special interest in us, we being a young couple and new parents. We enjoyed their fellowship, having great fun and laughter as we had them over for dinner in our apartment.

Pastor Crammer and Betty recommended that we being a young couple and I being young in the ministry—need to remember to spend quality time with each other for marriage enrichment. "Weekend getaways," they said, "were important and refreshing." They gave us recommendations to local hotel listings, places that they had enjoyed staying. What a special couple.

I shared with Pastor Ron Crammer some of the adjustment difficulties I was having, being a member of a "family church," like *Greater Hope*. Loving people, but often less than timely services, continual legalism, mediocrity. I did not know if there was any hope for *Greater Hope*.

Pastor Crammer encouraged us to visit New Mount Church, and we did. We always enjoyed the spirit-filled worship services. We eventually transferred our membership to New Mount Church where I became the youth minister. Colleen and I rented a very large, lovely apartment owned by the Crammers.

It was directly behind the church, which was both good and bad. At the conclusion of church services, guess where a lot of the young people hung out? Sure you're right, our place. Actually it was a lot of fun—not a lot of privacy, but a lot of fun. We started holding young adult bible studies in our home, "The Young Adults Cottage Bible Study," we called it.

I recalled the evening that we were scheduled to have the cottage Bible study. Colleen was now very pregnant with our second son. With multiple young people from church and family in our home, Colleen started having labor pains. I guess Colleen had not totally forgotten her first child-bearing experience (remember, *"Go get my mother!"*). She cried, "No, I don't want to go to the hospital!" Well, she and I did go. It was good timing, because six hours after our arrival at the hospital, the Lord blessed us once again with another son, Tyler Mozan Hendricks. The aftermath of the birth did bring some scare for Colleen and me. It was initially thought that Tyler had developed hydrocephalus (water on the brain). When I heard about the possibility, what came to my mind were twins who lived in Long Beach, who were said to have hydrocephalus. They had very large heads (extended foreheads). As I looked down at my beautiful child I thought, "no Lord, not Tyler, don't let this be."

Testing was completed, and it would take a week for the results. The week felt like an eternity. Colleen, holding Tyler, and I walked into the doctor's office, having that nervous feeling as we waited for him to enter the exam room.

Through our prayers and the prayers of many saints, we learned that it was misdiagnosed and Tyler went on to develop just fine. At the time of this writing, he is fifteen years old; in fact, he offered and is cooking Dad's breakfast. Today, being the typical fifteen-year-old boy, as I smell the breakfast cooking (Turkey hotdogs and eggs), he knows that I am writing about him in this section of the book. He is looking over my shoulder, saying, "Dad, man, why do you have to put me in your book?"

"Because it's my book!" The nerve of him to tell me who I should not put in my book! Boy, the life of parenting. And speaking of parenting, there came a period of my life that I was too tired to parent.

Too Tired to Parent

After graduating from California State University at Long Beach with a social work degree, I headed off to become a social worker, right? Wrong. Because my older brother, Leo, was the owner of two 7 Eleven stores, it was much easier to find employment at his Inglewood, California, store where I worked as a manager. The money was good but the hours were crazy and unpredictable, since it was a twenty-four hour retail operation. I also continued working as a Youth Minister at New Mount Church. This arrangement of working two jobs continued for five consecutive years, proving to be very costly physically, spiritually, and relationally. I had three homes: 7 Eleven, church, and my real home, the place where my wife and children lived, and where I mostly slept. At 7 Eleven I would often work fifty to sixty hours a week. Sometimes I would finish a shift and after arriving home, I would receive a phone call saying an employee did not show up for work, which meant I had to scramble to find a replacement or return to work the shift myself. Talk about the drama. I experienced "beer-runs"—folks grabbing six-packs of beers and then running out of the store. Once I caught a man stuffing ten packages of lunch meat inside the front of his pants, and the near robberies, I thank God He always helped me to avoid them. My beautiful wife never complained, but there were times I could sense the tension, especially when I was required to work on many holidays, even Christmas (good sales).

My children did not have a lot of interactions with me

other than play. I brought them their favorite fruit punch drinks and toys from the store to make me feel less guilty about being away from home so much.

I was not the strong disciplinarian; that was Colleen's role (very scriptural, right?); she spent more time with them after all. I was too busy managing a store, and too busy helping others at the church as a minister. The fact of the matter is that I would come home too tired to parent. Colleen, forced to do most of the disciplining of our two sons, was viewed by them as the mean person. The time that I did spend with them was in a playful role; they viewed me as the fun daddy, the fun teddy bear. For a minute I liked this "friend role." You will see why this role was so important to me later.

While managing the 7-Eleven store, there were two life-changing, dangerous, high drama, yet freeing, events that took place. The first involved a theft. I was on the store floor taking inventory when in walked a man approaching old age. He grabbed a cheap bottle of wine and ran out of the store without paying for it. At that moment, a burst of anger and energy circulated throughout my mind and body. I took off running after this man. That's right, out the door, down the street, and through the alley, the "store manager" is running after a wino with a bottle of wine dangling in his hands. It must have been a funny sight for people to behold.

Now in the alley and closing in on "Mr. Pitiful," I rehearsed the following in my head: "Who does he think he is, trying to out run me, a one-time sprinter turned marathoner?" As I was closing in on him, with the adrenaline flowing stronger, my thoughts continued, "He must not know who he is stealing from, he's taking from my brother, my blood. He don't know, I grew up in Compton, don't mess with me!"

I guess the man hearing and feeling my steps closing in on him, decided to suddenly stop. Now he was facing me, and I was facing him at an arm's length, and we are having a stare-down. I notice he is under the influence, as the foul smell of alcohol penetrated through his breath. In one final act of intimidation, the man raised the bottle of wine back towards his head, to gain force to hit me with it. With so much fight in me I was determined that this wino was not going to steal from me or injure me. As the bottle came down towards me, I grabbed it in mid-air from the man, while saying to him, "Give me that wine, you better get out of here!"

With that exchange, the man walked away, and I walked back towards the store, bottle of wine in my hand, coolness in my steps, saying to myself, "What's wrong with him, trying to steal some wine from me, not me!…not me!" Yes, I walked away, feeling good, but what a stupid thing to do, taking a chance like that. I did not know if the man had a gun or others working with him. Thank God for his protection. Let me fill you in on something else that infuriated and energized me to foolishly run after this man.

The man that I found myself running after had remarkably similar features to the man who molested me when I was eleven. Yes, this man with the Hispanic appearance had triggered a flashback of my molester, reliving his face; the sticky-sweet, foul smell of alcohol on his breath; his pores giving out the smell of cheap cologne mixed with sweat, which he had worn too many days. But on this day there was twist: what I could not do as a child, I could do as an adult. I could fight back, I could run. Yes, run after and run down what had been stolen from me, with no fear taking back what had been taken. Call it fate, call it stupid, call it dangerous, I called it God ordained, symbolic, and freeing.

The second life-changing, dangerous, high drama event was preceded by convictions already going on in my consciousness.

For me, I will say it again, for me, employment at 7-Eleven was not the right environment for me as a minister. Given what I had experienced through my life journey, my conscience was plagued by how I started viewing people.

Actually my "social work" mind of wanting to help people shifted. How did it shift? No one could be trusted; they all had the potential of taking advantage of a situation.

My conscience invoked, "Robert, how can you feel good about selling people *Playboy, Playgirl,* or *Hustler* magazines with all that filth which had plagued you? How can you feel good about selling folks alcohol and Zig Zag papers? You know most are not using it to roll tobacco!" I would try to deaden my Godly conscience by saying, "Yes Lord, but I am not forcing them to buy it, I am just providing a service, I am just ringing them up." Well, all of this was going on in my head, along with the too many hours away from my family, and I made the decision to seek employment elsewhere. The Lord made sure that I did not linger too long in my decision.

What started out as an uneventful day at the store would suddenly change. I was on the store floor stocking shelves, as we had earlier received a shipment of groceries. I really liked stocking the shelves since it made my day flow well not having to deal with customers, which had become less enjoyable. My sister was working the cash register that day, when suddenly I heard my name called, "Robert, I got a problem."

As I approached the cash register, she informed me that she had sold gasoline to a customer, not knowing he was going to pump the gas in a container non suitable for transporting gas. She had hit the emergency shut-off switch, disabling the pump and preventing the gentleman (I thought at the time) from proceeding. Having only been able to pump a small amount of the gas into the non-suitable container, he came storming back into the store to find out why the gasoline flow was suddenly stopped.

Well, guess who had the responsibility of explaining to him why he could not pump gas into a plastic milk container? Yes, you guessed it, "Mr. Store Manager."

As I tried to break it down to him why we were not allowed to sell him gas in the type of container he had, he was not hearing it.

Angrily, he said, "Why can't I get gas in this container?" Seconds after that, he took the small amount of gas that he had already pumped in the container and threw it in my face. My hands immediately went to my eyes as they burned with severe pain. For a moment I could do nothing but rapidly rub my eyes, unable to see. I did not know if the guy was going to inflict more harm on me, or even try to strike a match to set me on fire. I was happy to hear my sister say that "he had run out the store." Somehow I was able to feel my way to a wash basin to try irrigating my eyes, while at the same time I heard the siren of the paramedics that my sister had called to transport me to the hospital.

It was my first ride in an emergency response vehicle. Strapped in on the stretcher, heart beating fast, unable to see, the short ride to the hospital seemed so long—long enough to ponder the event. I questioned if I would be able to regain my sight, and I was reminded of concerns I was having about working at the convenience store. The Lord had once again gotten my attention, as he did when I was running from being a Minster, when He allowed me to get into the auto accident.

What followed were those famous words we have heard, "Lord, if you get me out of this…"

The Lord was gracious to me. Once in the emergency room, my eyes were irrigated with medical cleaning solutions which allowed me to regain my sight; I was discharged the same day. The man who threw the gas in my face was apprehended by the police a few days after the event as he walked across the store parking lot as if nothing had happened. Thank God for my sister's good description and security cameras. So, 7-Eleven was history, and I sought employment elsewhere. I was so relieved!

I landed a job first as a crisis phone counselor at a major chemical dependency and alcohol rehabilitation hospital. In reality, I felt more like an insurance screener, trying to hospitalize individuals who had good insurance that would cover a thirty-day stay, costing over thirty thousand dollars. For those who had no insurance but were ready to come in for treatment, I was required to give referrals to county treatment programs which could takes months for hospitalization due to a long waiting list. What a tragedy. This would only be short-term employment. At the end of the day, my performance was evaluated mainly by how many insured I talked into filling a hospital bed for thirty days. I felt more like a salesperson than a counselor.

I would later become a social worker and case manager for a senior service program in Long Beach, which was a very rewarding experience, and I would stay with this program for many years until I landed the job that I ultimately wanted. I became a medical social worker at Long Beach Memorial Medical Center, and my college dream became a reality. I continued working in this capacity until becoming a full-time Pastor. And how did I become a full-time Pastor? Well, it started in the Tehachapi Mountains.

The Shout!

For we do not have a high priest who is unable to sympathize with our weakness, but we have one who has been tempted in every way, just as we are—yet was without sin...
– Hebrews 4:15

Simon answered, "Master we've worked hard all night and haven't caught anything. But because you say so, I will let down the nets." – Luke 5:5

When I returned to Cal State University Long Beach, to finish my education, it was not a "cake walk." There were times that I wanted to once again hang up my education net. I felt I was working so much harder than my college classmates whose education was being paid for by their parents, who were not required to hold employment outside of going to school. This was certainly not the case for me. Accustomed to doing well in high school, it was a great disappointment when there were seasons in my college life that I would receive a series of non-passing grades following studying so hard. Was I trying too hard? Was I working too many hours trying to make ends meet? Discouragement began to speak. "Robert, quit, you don't need to be the first male in your family to earn a college degree. There are lots of guys who make a lot of money without a college degree, just quit." I am so glad that I did not succumb to those feelings.

I thank God that He showed up and encouraged me to change my thought pattern. He deepened my prayer life, increased my faith, shifted my thought patterns, no more "woe is me." He helped change my study habits and strengthened me when I was tired. Every once in awhile when I look at my college degree sitting on my bookshelf, I am full of gratitude to God!

Too Tired to Parent

> *...He welcomed them and spoke to them about the Kingdom of God, and healed those who needed healing. – Luke 9:11(b)*

I was the father who asked God to heal both of my sons because of birth complications, and He did. I was also the father who worked too much, making it impossible to make the impression God desired on their lives.

I struggled between work (including spiritual) and family. My employment took priority over being in position to teach my boys the guidelines, orderliness and the directives of the Lord. Yes, working so much, I was too tired to make the best godly impression on their lives, which should have been the opportune times at home, on outings, and before going to bed.

Despite the penalty I paid for not being there early in my boys' lives, I thank God that wisdom cried out and raised her voice. I heard, learned, and made changes. I cut back on work and started spending more time with my family. I thank God for my wife who took the disciplinarian helm in my absence, sometimes physically and sometimes emotionally. This certainly was not her primary responsibility. In addition I was not best fulfilling my marital vows "to cleave to my wife." I honor God for this spiritual awakening, realizing that my children and your children want structure and stability through discipline.

> *These are the commands, decrees and the laws the Lord your God directed me to teach you to observe in the land that you are crossing in the Jordan to possess, so that you and your children and their children after them may fear the Lord your God as long as you live by keeping all decrees and commands that I give you, and so that you might enjoy long life. Hear, O Israel, and be careful to obey so that it may go well with you and that you may increase greatly in a land flowing with milk and honey, just as the Lord, the God of your fathers, promised you.*
>
> *Hear, O Israel: The Lord our God, the Lord is one. Love the Lord your God with all your heart and with all your soul and*

with all your strength. These commandments that I give you today are to be upon your hearts. Impress them on your children. Talk about them when you sit at home and when you walk along the road, and when you lie down and when you get up. Tie them as symbols on your hands and bind them on your foreheads. Write them on the door frames of your houses and on your gates.
– Deuteronomy 6: 1-9 (NIV)

The fear of the Lord is the beginning of knowledge, but fools despise wisdom and discipline. Listen, my son, to your father's instruction and do not forsake your mother's teaching. They will be garlands to grace your head and a chain to adorn your neck.

Wisdom calls aloud in the street, she raises her voice in the public squares; at the head of noisy streets she cries out, in the gateways of the city she makes her speech.
– Proverbs 1: 7-9; 20-21 (NIV)

When a Giant Falls

The weekend was highly anticipated. I had told Pastor Crammer that I would be taking some time away with Colleen and friends (former members of New Mount Church), "going up to the mountains," I said. It would be one of those weekends away that he had so often encouraged. Pastor Crammer had assured me that there would be enough coverage for Sunday service, so off we went to the Tehachapi Mountains. It was a spectacular location, a mountain sanctuary, truly an enchanting place to take in. Laughter filled the car as we traveled and took in the beautiful California surroundings.

Ricky and Jackie McFarlin, along with Ivory Flowers (Jackie's sister), were our special friends whom we considered family. They were people with whom we could let our hair down, not needing to be on guard as to what we said, or how crazy we acted (we all need some of those friends in our lives). As we settled in and snuggled around the fireplace burning in the cozy cabin, we agreed that it was so nice to get away, to look at the vastness of God's creation. We ate, told funny stories, played games—it was such a high time. It was our joy that finally took us to a place of restfulness and off to sleep we all went that Friday night.

We awakened the next morning again with great anticipation of activities planned for the day. The smell of coffee, bacon, and eggs was a perfect delight to our senses as we stuffed ourselves with the hearty breakfast. It was a very cold day so we decided to stay indoors picking up where we left off the night before. It was a true "mountain" experience as we nestled around the fireplace. Yes, it was a "mountain" experience until we received a phone call from Mrs. Flowers, "Mother Flowers," as we liked to call her.

She gave us some disturbing news, news we could hardly

believe.

Pastor Crammer had died. "No, not Pastor Crammer; maybe it was his mother who had been sick for some time," were my first thoughts. Pastor Crammer had recently shared with the church congregation that he had just completed a physical, reporting his doctor saying "he was in good shape, that he just needed to eat less ice cream," his favorite dessert. We would receive a second phone call of confirmation. The reality was now sinking in; it was no mistake; Pastor Crammer, my giant with a limp, my mentor, had died of a sudden heart attack in his home. Yes, dead at the age of fifty-seven.

Our once "mountain" experience suddenly shifted to a "valley" experience—our emotions no longer high, we were feeling very low. Our laughter had turned to silence and tears as we snatched ourselves from denial into heartbroken reality. Our lives would be different without our Pastor Crammer. My life would be different in a big way, more than I could have imagined. As we prepared to travel down the mountain to meet those who were also grieving, I thought, "How would I find Betty Crammer, now the widow, and her children, and what would I say to bring comfort following this sudden and unexpected death?" As the youth minister, what would I say to the congregation who would be without their Pastor for the first time? It would be something to sleep on.

The next day on Sunday, we made the emotional journey down the mountain back to Los Angeles.

Colleen and I made a quick stop at home to unpack and then drove to the Crammer's home to offer our condolences and to comfort the family. As we arrived at the home, Colleen and I sat in the car for a moment to collect our thoughts, which felt like they were running in slow motion. We prayed that God would give us the right reaction when we would see the family and others visiting; that he would give us the right words to say. We noticed many cars parked on both sides of the street, which meant to us that we would be walking into a home filled with people.

As I opened the door to get out of the car, I turned on my strong spiritual clergy persona and compartmentalized my grief as Colleen and I walked into the Crammers' home.

We walked into the living room, which was filled with the immediate family and church members. As we made our rounds to the arms of loved ones, tearing and holding us with tight embraces, we all struggled to make sense of this sudden life-changing event.

The widow sitting almost in the middle of the living room retold the event over and over to each new arrival to the home. I thought, how insensitive of people to almost demand that she re-live, re-tell the story of how Pastor Crammer departed this life.

When the room was hushed with silence as grieving individuals collected their thoughts, eyes seemed to be focused on me to say something spiritual, to bring comfort. That night I did not want to act out the "spiritual giant." I wanted to grieve, but in my head that would be less than spiritual for this occasion.

I said the things that "deep Christians" say when a saint dies, "God is still in control. We don't understand His timing, but we need to accept that His timing is right; God will help us through this time."

As Colleen and I traveled home from the Crammers', something was captivating my heart, a premonition that God would be ushering me into a greater leadership capacity at New Mount Church. Was I being too premature? Should I even be thinking about who would be taking the reins of the pastorate before the "Home Going" service had taken place? I was already reluctant to accept that which yet had not been offered. At the time of Pastor Crammer's death, there were four associate ministers along with one military chaplain to whom Pastor Crammer had been acting as advisor. I rationalized that God could ordain one of them to take the pastorate if He so desired. Trust me, there were at least two of them who would turn flips to get the call, which would come from the church presiding officer, Bishop Kent Day. I tried to erase the thought out of my mind, but God was preparing me for the nod. I had apprehension, yet my obedience was required.

Late Sunday evening, I received a phone call from Bishop Kent Day. "Robert, this is Bishop Day, how are you doing fella? Robert, I need for you to be the interim, you know, the interim pastor." The call that I felt would come, came. With my acceptance followed a roller coaster of emotions, egos, expectations, and exhaustion. Would it be his shoes, my shoes, or God's shoes?

His Shoes, My Shoes, or God's Shoes?

Once the information trickled down to the ministerial staff that I had been appointed the interim pastor, there was a noticeable shift in relationship and personality with two ministers, as hurt and jealousy raised their ugly heads. I could read it on their facial expressions. I could hear it in their communication, even as I was careful to emphasize a team spirit.

Grief is an emotional response to loss with many stages, and boy was that evident of the widow of Pastor Crammer who was obviously having difficulty accepting the loss. You could read it on her face, which projected deep sadness; it was in her voice, as I recall having a bereavement conversation with her. With tears she said to me, "I no longer know what to do." I reassured her that there was still a place for her at the church, which included continuing to teach the new members class she so much enjoyed. I also told her there was no rush to clean her husband's office, as I knew the experience would no doubt be heartwrenching. Not long after this conversation, I noticed a marked difference in the widow's personality; she became more visible, more active, and at times more abrupt in her conversation with others and with me. At times she gently reminded me how her husband would handle certain tasks and circumstances. At times, I viewed the reminders as helpful insight, while at other times if felt more like tools of persuasion.

There were other members who tried to give helpful support by saying, "I am praying for you. I know you have some big shoes to fill."

I cringed inside as I thought, "I am not interested in filling anyone's shoes; there was enough uncertainty about the size of my own shoes to handle so much drama that was unfolding." My prayer was, "Lord, help my loved ones to accept that Pastor Crammer is now in your presence, unable to shepherd your church from the grave, through me or anyone else."

There were three events that pushed my spiritual buttons during the period of my interim pastorate:

It was obvious to me that the widow was in the race to not let the founder's legacy die. She had an urgency to establish a library in honor of her husband, Dr. Ron Crammer, Jr. It was a noble gesture to consider, but there had been no discussion with me, the interim pastor. I only found out about the library plans when I was made aware that there was a truck driver waiting to deliver shelving for a library that had not been planned. I instructed the messenger to inform the truck driver that we would not be accepting his delivery. It would be my first reality check to the widow. I informed her that she did not have the liberty to bring any new phases to the church without my consultation and blessings. I was not reading her venture as a reaction from grief; but rather I saw it as control motivated.

The Robe

The military chaplain for whom Pastor Crammer had acted as advisor would stay in our fold for awhile. I am certain he was dealing with a deep level of grief. His presence made my journey as interim pastor very challenging.

This was a very multi-talented young man. He was quite an accomplished pianist and vocalist. In addition, he wore a level of charisma with the ability to hold an audience when articulating a sermon. He had even been an out-of-state pastor. It was not his abilities that made this chaplain a challenge for me, nor did I feel he was envious of my position. I had known this chaplain over the years as he had grown up in The Church of Christ Holiness U.S.A. It was hard for him to stay in one place for any length of time. His employment was no exception. I would have long periods of not seeing or hearing from the chaplain, and then he would just "pop up" unannounced and share all the spectacular and luxurious activities of his life. There was certainly a component of this chaplain's lifestyle that was curious at best. His self-confidence often came close to cockiness or arrogance.

Until the time of Pastor Crammer's death, the chaplain and I had an amiable relationship; but his actions after the death would prickle our interaction. I perceived his actions as taking advantage of a situation and causing spiritual chaos for an already grieving church membership. The chaplain thought spending more time at the church would bring more comfort and confidence to me in my new role. It might have if he had not stuck with me like glue, sharing how much Pastor Crammer meant to him but mostly telling me about his many contacts and relationships.

He was a leader of a men's group that assisted men in recapturing their identity and bringing out their best through weekend gatherings in various locations throughout the country. There would be times that my ministry preparation would be stymied—I tried not to appear disinterested in the Chaplain's conversation, which seemed so important to him but a hindrance to me. I guess you could say that I was a great big sponge. There were times that I was tempted to park my car a block from the church or not show up at the church office for ministry preparation for the fear of being sidetracked.

I recall a conversation with Pastor Crammer when he was living about some of the interesting things people do when a church leader dies. I particularly recall him talking about some of the ritual practices certain black churches held when a Pastor or Deacon died. The membership believes that it is appropriate to make it off limits to have anyone sit in the seat of the deceased for a period of time. Sometimes they would drape it with some covering. Frankly, we both chuckled about how strange we thought this was, the extent people would go to try to remember a person who was dead. I remembered him saying that he did not want this fuss for him, and I agreed with the same thoughts for myself.

I was shocked to enter the pulpit area one Sunday to find the chair in which Pastor Crammer had sat draped with his robe. It gave the appearance of a throne not to be touched or sat in. I was taken back to the conversation Pastor Crammer and I had about the strangeness of the remembrance.

My first reaction was turmoil. Who would do such a thing? Maybe I was overreacting; perhaps it was needed to bring comfort to the widow and possibly others. Well, I had made the decision to live with it for a period of time, being careful not to sit in the "sacred seat" and not even to ask who was responsible for the act of memorial. My restraint lasted for about three weeks. I could take it no longer, and one weekday when I was at the church alone, I entered the pulpit, took the robe from the chair, and hung it up in the office closet. It is time to move on from this morbid ritual, I thought, especially since it was against Pastor Crammer's desires. I had made the decision that although the robe would be removed, I would not sit in the chair, so that folks would not mistake the actions for my being anxious to become the pastor. Sunday would roll around, and it would be the first time that members would see the robe no longer draped on the former Pastor's chair. We got through the service with no noticeable reaction by the saints, but after the service I walked by a few of the saints, you know the "pillars of the church" as we sometimes call them. I heard one of them whispering as I went by, "What happened to the robe?" Who removed it?" It was somewhat humorous, because they were not coming directly to me to ask, and boy was I waiting for the question.

Yes, I was ready to give a response and eager to ask a few questions of my own, questions like, "Who draped the robe over the chair, and who gave permission to do so?"

I had a strong suspicion that it was the military chaplin who felt so spiritually endowed to make such a memorial gesture in displaying the robe. The military chaplain decided it was time to move on to the next journey, and he left the church a reminder that he had graced our presence. What was that reminder? The widow of Pastor Crammer would bring to my attention a phone bill with excessive long distance calls the military chaplain made, not seeking permission, nor offering compensation. My lasting impression of the military chaplain was a powerful young man in whom God was doing a work in his life, if he would just settle down and stop running from his shadow.

Pregnant Moments

It was now close to one year that I had been acting as the interim pastor. One Saturday morning I was working in the office, when the sound of a knock came at the door. It was a Deacon who asked if I could join him and other Deacons downstairs in the Church's overflow room. They were discussing future plans for the pastorate. There was one Deacon who expressed "feeling uncomfortable with my presence at this stage of their meeting." This was short-lived as the other Deacons expressed their approval of my presence.

As I sat around the table with the other leaders I wondered, what's going on that required me to be summoned and why was this one Deacon so alarmed by my being invited to their meeting? Following a period of small talk and the exchange of niceties, we came to the crux of the meeting. The appointed spokesperson of Deacons conveyed to me that they were at the point of seeking a pastor for the church and wanted to know if I would be willing to take the position at their recommendation. All eyes were on me as I paused to take in what was being asked of me. It was one of those pregnant moments as the partial smiles on the Deacons' faces expressed confidence that I would graciously accept their offer. What they did not know was I already had a premonition that the offer would be made. The work that God had begun in me was not finished, He had already told me that accepting the pastorate at this stage of His work in me was not in His plan. I thanked the Deacons for their vote of confidence in me, and then I voiced that it was not God's timing for me to become the pastor of New Mount Church. The room was swallowed up in silence. The Deacons, including the one who initially felt uncomfortable with my attending the meeting, radiated shock in their demeanor that I turned down the position. It was as if they thought it would be a slam-dunk, who would not want to be the pastor of such a church with its legacy and future potential?

Regaining their composure slowly, it was decided that they would consult with the Bishop in seeking a search committee to include announcing nationally that the pastorate at New Mount Church was open.

The search was on, and resumes from interested pastoral candidates locally and from across the country began to trickle in. Following the review of many resumes, the final prospects included two local pastors and two out-of-state pastors. One particular candidate named Agen Depart, who was pastoring a church in Chicago, Illinois, was an interest to some, as he had conducted a revival at our church about a week prior the death of Pastor Crammer. He was a young man who exemplified a great deal of "bang" in his sermon delivery, often pacing and twisting as if prancing through a dance, as his voice tone through the sermons reached a crescendo.

The Unveiling

His style had certainly made an impression on many of the parishioners at New Mount Church. Candidly, I did not share the same impression; I guess you could say I was having difficulty grasping the spiritual substance from what appeared to be performance, as the saying goes, "A lot of smoke but no steak."

Nonetheless, it was a lasting impression that gave him a front seat in being the favorite candidate for the pastorate.

As the pastoral selection reached its final stages, to say that the process became political is an understatement. While we emphasized, "that the process should be seasoned with prayer, asking God for His guidance in selection," there were certain "pillars of the church" helping God by manipulating the process—forming lobbies to support their favorite candidate. It went as far as individuals going through the membership roster to contact members who were not frequent in church attendance, to beg of them to be present during the special election meeting for the final voting on the next pastor of New Mount Church.

The stage was set; the Saturday morning for a decision had come. It was amazing, as I scanned the congregation of God's people, the sanctuary was practically full. Saints were there that I had not seen in a long while; frankly there were some folks present that I did not know were members. It would come down to three candidates on the secret ballot, as one of the strong candidates had requested that his name be pulled out of the process because he and his family could not live on the financial package offered. Final ballot instructions were given by the pastoral search committee, and the voting took place.

Once the votes were tabulated the next pastor of New Mount Church would be Agen Depart of Chicago. As the results were announced, many of the parishioners were smiling and celebrating, but not I. I was happy that the process was over, but my heart was heavy with a discernment that all would not be well with New Mount because of the selection. The search committee would be contacting the other candidates, thanking them for their interest, and making the first official contact with Pastor Agen Depart to congratulate him. When the call was made, he had already been contacted by one of the lobbyists.

Arrangements were made to relocate Pastor Agen Depart and his family to Los Angeles. My heart remained heavy over the selection. I questioned why I was having theses feelings. It was I who had made it clear to the Deacons that it was not God's timing that I would take the position, and the people had spoken; so get over it Robert, were my thoughts. But I was still having a hard time with the decision my loved ones had made. During one of my study times, God captured my mind with the scriptures in *1 Samuel 8,* when Israel wanted a king to lead them.

> The Lord told Samuel, to listen to them and give them a King. The Lord impressed me with what He told Samuel, *Now listen to them: but warn them solemnly and let them know what the king who will reign over them will do.* – 1 Samuel 8:9 (NIV)

I did share my concerns privately with some of Deacons, emphasizing that they remain prayerful and careful with the pastor who was on his way.

It was comforting to me that I was able to free myself by

sharing my thoughts with the Deacons, but what followed was an overwhelming prompting by God that my family and I would soon be leaving New Mount Church. Prior to Pastor Depart's arrival, I had written a congratulatory letter which included my availability to show him around and fill him in on some of the church dynamics. I thought this would allow for a smooth transition.

At the pastor's arrival, we exchanged friendly greetings followed by my handing him the letter. I waited a week or two, never to hear any acknowledgement of the letter's content. I am not the brightest guy, but his non-response felt like he was saying, "I don't need your help." The prompting of God to end our stay at New Mount Church was even stronger. It would be the best decision to combat divided loyalties among the members, and in addition, to solve the uneasiness I felt about the new pastor. There was just something about this new pastor that did not sit well with me. I definitely was feeling that my loved ones would be getting more than what they bargained for!

The church would give my family and me an appreciation service, which was a wonderful send off. We departed following a twenty-year stay with the church, with no plans of returning. We were not even certain if we would remain with the denomination. Another chapter in my life had ended. The departure brought a season of soul searching, wheels of emotions, amazement and freedom. My family and I would attend a church in Hermosa Beach, California, called Hope Chapel.

It felt so different not sitting in a pulpit, we were surrounded by people dressed very casually, and best of all, they did not know who we were. The service reminded me of church services I had attended way back when I was in high school. No choir, just a few guys on the platform with guitars and good sounding voices leading the worshippers in singing. The pastor of the church entered the platform area also dressed casually, and bringing a great teaching-style message. As I sat there taking in the whole experience, I felt a degree of guilt that I, a minister and former interim pastor, was being ministered to as opposed to ministering. Go figure, such bondage, is that crazy or what? We attended Hope Chapel a few more times, along with some other churches, which were all good for our souls. We also stayed home some Sundays and rested. We called those times, "Mount Pillow of Rest, and Sweet Home."

The word got out that I was no longer the interim pastor and member of New Mount Church. Within a fairly short period of time, I would receive offers to consider pastorates at churches in Kansas City, Indiana, and California. I turned down all offers not feeling the peace or blessing of God. There was a sense that God was shielding me from disaster of accepting these offers, without His refining my life further.

It did not take long for the thrill of being able to get up any given Sunday, free to attend whatever church I wanted, to be gone. It was replaced with the feeling of being out of place, on the sideline of Ministry.

Unsettled about making a commitment to any given church and worried about my family not having a place to call their church home, I gradually broke down to seek guidance and encouragement from two brothers-in-law who were both members of the clergy and members of the same church organization. My phone call to Robert Winn, who at that time was a pastor of a church in San Francisco, supported my decision of leaving my prior church to alleviate conflict. My phone call to my brother Lindsay Emery, who was a pastor in Chicago and presiding officer within the denomination, was equally helpful by suggesting that I unite with an affiliated church, Zion Temple Cathedral Church in Los Angeles. He further recommended that I make myself available for ministry opportunities until God led me otherwise; in other words, a place where my family and I could rest our coats. It was a welcome suggestion and affirmed by Colleen. I must say Zion Temple Cathedral Church membership took some getting accustomed to.

Unlike our previous membership at New Mount Church, Zion Temple Cathedral Church had a largely older membership with the sprinkling of a few youth and young adults. Over the years at New Mount we had developed an appreciation for an upbeat contemporary style of music and singing. This was not the style at Zion Temple, where the music department trademarks were hymns and anthems. I recall our first Sunday of worship, my youngest son Tyler in his stuttering voice asked me, "Dad, wh-where are the drums?" I explained to him that this church did not have drums.

As we looked around the congregation, we witnessed many older ladies adorned in hats, small and large, and some were gigantic. One thing for certain, it might have been a different style of worship, but God was praised as they opened their mouths to sing, and their smiles radiated the love of Jesus as they welcomed our family into their fellowship.

Once Colleen and I, along with our children, simmered in the newness of the church environment, we fell in love with the people, and we felt that love reciprocated. Colleen and I both taught Sunday school classes. In addition, I began to teach Bible study and eventually become the assistant pastor. So much for feeling out of sync and un-connected.

In the meanwhile, I continued to work full time as a medical social worker at Long Beach Memorial Hospital.

Take My Run Away?

While Serving at Zion Temple Cathedral Church, my life would change in such a supernatural way, by God's miraculous allowance and order. I had started running marathons in the mid 80's, and had completed many. I continued my running even while serving at Zion Temple Cathedral Church. The 26.2 miles runs grew on me as I looked forward to training for them throughout the year. That meant getting up at crazy hours of the morning to get training runs in. Rain or shine, I was out on the street or beach running while normal people were sleeping. I had made changes to my diet to get "mean and lean." I remember my sister-in-law, who had not seen me for awhile, saying to me, "You look like you have AIDS," because I had lost so much weight in training. Besides the endorphins high and the desire to feel fit, why had I taken up running marathons? I was a sprinter in my early years, why did I turn to distance running?

I ran because I could run; yes, I could run long and hard to escape, even for a moment, life's tensions. It was linked to accomplishments, and running out the unfinished business of my childhood trauma. I could not run then, but now I had enough endurance to run my personal best, to see the trees, to see the sky, to see the ocean, to remind myself that building endurance was a process. I recalled when I first started training I could not run a half a block without being out of breath. I kept at it with determination, and before long it got easier and easier—half a mile turned into a mile, a mile turned into two miles, and so on. While running, I was thanking God for all the detours of my life, and yet there was still a distance to go, I had not made it to the finish line yet. I learned by running marathons that there are hills, flat surfaces, and sometimes the unexpected. In real life, I was about to experience the unexpected which would lead me into a period of depression.

I had been diagnosed with glaucoma for several years now, with my ophthalmologist trying to control the pressure behind my optic nerve with ophthalmic medications and laser surgeries, with no good or lasting results. Following multiple medical consultations, the decision was made to undergo a more aggressive type of glaucoma surgery in my right eye (place of highest pressure) called Trabeculectomy. My wife and I would arrive at the outpatient surgery center on an early June morning. I started to get a little nervous when I was asked to fill out an Advance Directive (I highly recommend in light of Terri Schiavo case/2005) in case of complications during the surgery. I thought, "complication on eye surgery?" Oh well.

I was told to get undressed and relax on the gurney until the anesthesiologist came. As I tried to relax, I began to view my medical wrist band and my heart dropped when I noticed they had the wrong spelling of my last name. I quickly jumped off the gurney and ran for the nurse. "Hey, Hey, I want to make sure you are going to perform the right surgery on me, because you have the wrong last name on my medical identification band. I am here for glaucoma surgery on my right eye." After checking the medical file/doctor's orders, it was determined that the nurse had just misspelled my name on the wrist band. She had spelled it Hendrix, instead of Hendricks (not for the first time, I guess some think I should be related to Jimmy Hendrix).

My wife had a big laugh after it was over, but it was not funny at the time. I remember while growing up, a friend's father went into the hospital to have one of his legs amputated, and they amputated the wrong leg—true story.

It would be a surgery that would take a few hours, allowing me to be released from the hospital the same day. It would require me to wear a patch on my right eye for thirty days while healing. I had lifting restrictions. I was also prohibited from working for a month. During the healing process, having the use of only one eye, I could really appreciate those who were born or became blind. There were periods when I contemplated what it would be like if I lost my sight completely, how would that change my life. I never dwelt on it for long periods, but I understood that it could be the reality for me someday. It made me consider how important it was to take time to look at God's beautiful creation, take in sunsets, notice the spectacular flowers, appreciate the walks and runs on the beach.

Speaking of runs, I was anxious to get back to training for the next Los Angeles Marathon. So thirty days had passed since the surgery, and I would be seeing my ophthalmologist for my first post-operation exam. As I sat in the examination chair waiting for the doctor to arrive, I was anxious, yes anxious to hear him say the surgery was a success and that I could get back to a normal life.

As he removed the patch from my eyes and with his ophthalmic medical equipment, he looked into my eye, "Look up, look down, look over my shoulder, focus on that mirror just behind me." He followed by saying, "Fine you can sit back now." He wrote a few things in my chart and then came the moment I had been waiting for. He said the surgery was a success. He told me that I would still have to watch my lifting of any heavy objects for a while, and that I should not participate in any contact recreation that could cause injury to my eyes.

He further told me that I would be free to return to work. The report was a sweet sound to my ears, as I thanked him for the good news. I further told him that I was so glad to be able to get back to my marathon training.

My doctor exclaimed, "marathon training?"

"Yes, I run marathons."

He said, "Robert, with the type of surgery you have undergone, you will not be able to do distance running."

I thought I was in a dream world, that I did not hear him clearly. As I sat there in a funk, I said, "What do you mean?"

He explained to me that the type of surgery I had was to bring my optic pressure below normal (which was desirable given my glaucoma history); therefore, any constant pounding such as distance running could cause a detached retina, which would lead to loss of sight.

I could not believe what I was hearing. I was at a loss for words, stunned. Why did he not tell me this prior to surgery? Why did I not ask? Why would I ask? What does eye surgery have to do with running?

As I sat there frustrated and near tears, I could only say, "I see." As I walked to my car following the appointment, my inner voice said, "If I would have only known, I would have elected to not have the surgery even though I might have gone blind." When I arrived home, my wife could sense by my face and quiet spirit that something had gone wrong. "Honey, he said I can't run marathons anymore."

She tried her best to comfort me, but I found myself quickly fading into a bout of depression. For that day, the unexpected happened to me. It brought on a childhood flashback of when, because of scoliosis, I had to stop running.

My other loved ones tried to cheer me up by suggesting that I start walking as it was less stressful on my body, "Robert what about cycling, that's a good sport?"

"No, I don't want to walk, I don't want to ride. If I can't run marathons, I don't want to do anything." No more viewing running magazines, no more watching marathons, no exercise at all for a while, was the reality of the depression that set in.

I guess you can say, "You can box in an athletic person just for so long." As I began to notice the many photos of myself running L.A. Marathons and the completion medals displayed around the house, it finally hit me. "How many people could say that they ran even one marathon?" I had completed many and had the proof to back it. God used what was visible to me, sparking the realization of accomplishment, to slowly bring me out of the funk of depression. I realized that being physically inactive was doing more to hurt myself than good, as I began to take on extra body weight. I could no longer focus on "water under the bridge."

I don't want to leave the impression that it was an easy task of making the adjustment. On several follow-up appointments with my ophthalmologist, I would ask my doctor, "Are you sure that I can't distance run ever?" In his monotone voice, he informed me that I would be taking a risk if I did. Boy, did I want to get out of the examining chair and choke him! Just kidding. On one of my visits when I brought up the issue, I sensed that he had anticipated the question, and with mild frustration in his voice he said, "It would be okay if you ran 4-5 miles a few times per week, but no more than that." It was a kind of bittersweet response.

I was glad that he said I could run, but I wanted to run more than he recommended. In addition, I was still a little fearful to even run the 4-5 miles, because maybe I was still setting myself up for a detached retina. Maybe I pulled from my doctor an approval that he only gave to stop me from bugging him. I must say I have been faithful to not running more than his recommended miles; in fact, it has been far less because of my apprehension.

Eventually, I did buy a bike. It sat in my garage for almost a year until my son started using it. I was not about to become a world class cyclist. What would grow on me was walking, not speed walking; that looks too silly. But walking at a fairly good pace, and taking in all the God-given surroundings; and wouldn't you know it, walking now is just as meaningful to me as running marathons used to be.

From A CRY To A SHOUT

The Shout!

> *Do you not know that in a race all the runners run, but only one gets the prize? Run in such a way as to get the prize. Everyone who competes in the games goes into strict training. They do not get a crown that will last forever. Therefore I do not run like a man running aimlessly: I do not fight like a man beating the air. No I beat my body and make it my slave so that after I have preached to others, I myself will not be disqualified for the prize. – 1 Corinthians 9: 24-27*

I thank God for life lessons. I had trained many years and completed many marathons. When I received the bad news from my ophthalmologist that I could no longer run marathons, the emotional pain was great as I pitied myself. My pain was great enough to not just affect me, but those I loved. I can now celebrate God's course for my life, as He used my history of running marathons to continue aiding me in running my life's journey. What was key was moving beyond my emotional pain. The physical transferred to the spiritual. I transferred my thought of continuing running for a prize, for a crown that would last forever. With even greater intensity, I trained with God's Word being the training plan. Yes, the course had been changed, and I wanted to be victorious. I want to be able to say I have fought a good fight, I have finished my course, I have kept the faith. Thank God there is a crown of righteousness, *which the Lord the righteous shall Judge, shall give me at that day and not me only, but unto all them also that love his appearing. – 2 Timothy 4:7,8.*

Praise God for using my participation in marathons as a reminder of the miles I had already completed in my life journey: the experience of an alcoholic father, the death of my oldest brother, the shame of being sexually molested, the two near-death encounters, the scoliosis experience, the pornography trap, the death of my mentor, and the darkness of my glaucoma surgery. Each experience a marathon in and of itself. Sometimes hilly, sometimes flat, sometimes the feeling of "hitting the wall," sometimes feeling like getting out of the race. I am so glad that I stopped at the water station of God's Holy word which refreshed, reestablished my endurance, and brought me back into focus on the finish line. On your way to the finish line, the unexpected can occur.

Beat The Press

God's timing is simply amazing. As I arrived at Long Beach Memorial Medical Center, I would be greeted by my supervisor. "Robert, I wanted to know if you would be interested in being interviewed by my daughter?" My supervisor informed me that her daughter was a journalist for the *Los Angeles Times*, a major newspaper. She needed to interview married couples with children regarding parenting. "Can you help her out?"

"Sure," I responded. I received a phone call from my supervisor's daughter that weekend, introducing herself as Ference Sky. She explained the focus of the interview. There was the possibility that the interview would be published. With my approval we began the interview over the telephone.

At the start of the interview she obtained basic information such as my place of residence, marital status, my age, and names of my wife and children. The meat of the interview questions surrounded parenting styles. I expressed to my interviewer that, "If I am honest with myself I would say Colleen, my wife, is the strong disciplinarian in our home." I continued by stating, "I devoted too much time helping others as a minister and social worker, and not enough time with my two boys," who at that time were 11 and 5. I also expressed to her that "I was inclined to give my sons time-outs or take privileges from them as an easier form of discipline." Ference's follow-up question led to a spectacular admission, an answer that would release the quiet storm held in for so many years. She asked me why I embraced my style of parenting?

As I relaxed there on the bed, lying on my back with my eyes focused on the ceiling, shamelessly I told her that my style of parenting was the result of my poor relationship with my father who was an alcoholic. I told her "If I had a close relationship with my father, I would have been able to tell him that I had been sexually molested when I was 11-years old. I wanted to be certain that my sons can tell me anything." What the interviewer did not know was I had yet to tell anyone in my family other than Colleen of the sexual abuse. It was an outrageous moment, I had spilled my heart, shared my secret held in all these years. Following the revelation, the butterflies in my stomach were flying, as my heart skipped beats. The panic was on, as thoughts rolled over in my mind, "What would happen if a family member picked up a copy of the *Los Angeles Times* and read that I was sexually abused as a child?" As the interview concluded, I was cautiously relieved as Ference Sky reminded me that there would be no guarantee that the interview would ever be published.

The release of tension was short-lived, as some days later I received a phone call from Mark Tanner, a photographer for the *L.A. Times*. He requested an appointment to take pictures of the family and me, in the event that the story would go to the press. At the photographer's arrival, once again he reiterated that his taking the photographs was no guarantee that the story would be printed. "Yeah, sure," I thought to myself. About a week later the suspense was over as I received a call from Ference Sky informing me that in fact the article would be featured in the *L.A. Times*.

A rush flowed through my body, a resolve to gather my family together to break the news of my molestation which had been tucked away all these years. It would come down to a newspaper article that would spring me into action. A plan of action is what I needed to tell my family before August 31, 1994, the date the article would hit the newsstand.

God's provision and timing are dramatic as he gave me insight to arrange meetings with my family during the week of the Ninety-eighth Church of Christ (Holiness) national convention held at the Burbank Airport Hilton Hotel, in California. The theme of the convention was:

Embracing the vision to receive the Victory Habakkuk 2:2

The national convention was held a little more than a week prior to the article hitting the newsstands. I had notified my family in advance that I wanted to share something with them. We would meet in the suite-size room of my brother-in-law, Bishop Emery Lindsay, and sister Pearl Lindsay. This was a perfect arrangement, as most of my family members, with the exception my father, would be attending the evening service. Bishop Lindsay would be bringing the sermon that Sunday evening. His message was such a segue to what I would be sharing with the family after the sermon. The title of his message was, *"David Recovered All,"* 1 Samuel 30:1-16. From this passage of scripture, he nailed home the following three points:

1. *Before David could recover, he had to lose all.*
2. *Many times, the crisis we face brings us closer to God.*
3. *Three things the modern Church needs in order to thrive: vision, passion, and God-inspired action.*

A Happy Time Coming

My brother-in-law would conclude the message by calling for the closing song: *"There's a Happy Time A-Coming."*

That evening, God had already allowed me to embrace the hurt of my childhood molestation, but shortly I would be embracing the victory of releasing my hidden story of 26 years for the first time with my family.

That evening, I would be losing all my reservations and

secrecy to recover full transparency. As I meditated on the message, my confidence and anticipation mounted as I was feeling so much at peace with God, and yes, I could agree that my crisis had brought me closer to God.

I could visualize a happy time coming following the God-inspired action I would complete. The service would end, and my family and I would make our way to the room on that Sunday evening, August 14, 1994.

As my mother, sisters, and brothers gathered in the room, I was ripe for the moment. I scanned the room to find the atmosphere very tranquil. The faces of my loved ones were very serious and anticipating, projecting that I was about to drop something serious on them. I began my talk by telling my family that I was in a good place, and I was not seeking their pity for something about which they had no knowledge or control.

I further informed them of the urgency of telling them about my childhood trauma. With full composure I began, "When I was eleven I was sexually molested by Ramón in Mexicali…" When I finished the story, there were tears from the eyes of some of my sisters, with expressions of shock and difficulty understanding how I could keep this tragedy in for many years. What a release for me; the weight of my emotions were as light as a feather. As I inwardly thanked God for the circumstances that led to the unveiling, I regretted my father was not present to hear my story with the rest of my family. The experience was a boost of confidence for sharing the same information with my father the next day. I had already anticipated that my father would be in denial and questioning why I would wait until I was an adult to break this news, but he did not let me down. It did not matter at this point how he would accept the event, but that he would be the last family member to share my saga before running my victory lap in overcoming the years, crying and exchanging it for a shout.

On the morning of August 31, 1994, the calls began to

flood in. "I read your story in the *Los Angeles Times*." Yes, there it was a large, full-color picture of my youngest son and me. With the caption beneath, "Robert Hendricks spends some time with his son Tyler, 5. Hendricks, 37, used to "come home too tired to be a parent, so he was a pal to his two boys."

I hurriedly perused "The Friend Trend" article to find out just what they said about my molestation, and there it was, much less than I thought, "...as a child, I could never talk to my alcoholic father. I wanted so badly to tell him that I had been sexually abused, but I never could. I wanted to make sure that my sons could tell me anything."

Freedom Sunday

There was a young man who had received notification that the king had died. This king had started strong, but allowed arrogance to capture his life. God struck the king with leprosy, and succumbing to this disease, he died. Once this young man heard of the king's death, he suddenly felt overwhelmed, burdened, and empty.

This young man took his burden down to the temple and began to meditate on God. A death caused the young man to seek God in the temple. In the year that this king died, he saw the Lord. God supernaturally lifted this young man up in the spirit, beyond Jerusalem, beyond the empty throne of the once-king. The young man was taken to the throne room in heaven; it was there that he saw God on His throne, high and lifted up; His throne filled the temple. There still in the spirit realm, the young man witnessed ministering spirits, angels, seraphims surrounding the throne.

They broke out in a song, singing "HOLY, HOLY, HOLY IS THE LORD GOD OF HOSTS, THE WHOLE EARTH IS FILLED WITH HIS GLORY." The young man cried, "Woe is me, for I am a man undone…" The young man was in the best place to make this confession, in the presence of God. God said, so to speak, "Angels at my service, I need you to help my child today, go over to the altar and pick up a live coal of fire. Touch the young man's lips, and tell him that he is going to be all right. Tell him that his sins are forgiven and his iniquity purged. "After the young man was touched and made whole, he heard God saying, "Whom shall I send and who will go for us? "The young man said," HERE AM I, SEND ME." — *Isaiah 6:1-8*

At last, Sunday morning service at Zion Temple Cathedral Church in Los Angeles, California. I noticed from the pulpit parishioners gathering and going to their normal seats, and the choir members taking their regular places in the choir stand. What started off as a typical service certainly would not end that way. It would be a service that evidenced true spiritual emancipation for me.

There had been many, many church services in which I felt less than free to praise God. Call it sophistication, call it shyness, or call it being "bound," the term "spiritual folks" like to use. I liken the experience to joy in a corked bottle, waiting to be released, and I was ready to place all of my reservations in the hands of the Holy Spirit to uncork my joyful praise. I had finally reached the light at the end of a tunnel. In rapid succession, there were my memories of God tenderly giving me victory over the hurt of being exposed to an alcoholic father, being sexually molested, seeing me through scoliosis and spinal surgery, shielding me from death, delivering me from pornography, ushering me into sharing childhood secrets, and safeguarding me through Glaucoma surgery. The season was right for the bottle to be uncorked. When a dear sister finished giving her utmost in a song of praise, the cork was released. The Holy Ghost had filled me with Joy overflowing and for the first time but certainly not the last, my hands went vertical and shouts flowed from my lips, as I gave praises and thanksgiving to God my Deliverer. The experience infiltrated the congregation as my beloved joined in with my rejoicing. The experience will forever be the landmark of my spiritual freedom.

Irreconcilable for Him, Reconcilable for Me

God brought back to my mind the Saturday morning that I met with the Deacons at New Mount Church to disclose to them that it was not God's timing for me to accept their offer of the pastorate. God further ushered to my memory, the helpful conversation I had with my brother-in-law, Bishop Emery Lindsay, who suggested I unite with Zion Temple Cathedral Church until God led me elsewhere.

I and my family were now in our fifth year at Zion Temple Cathedral Church, with all the amazement of God's timing and spiritually growing through God's permissible circumstances. Who would have ever thought that these five years away from New Mount Church would bring such tender contentment?

We were feeling so much love from the people of Zion Temple Cathedral Church, and we felt we were impacting their lives as well.

I recalled the uneasiness I had about Pastor Agen Depart as the replacement of Pastor Rod Crammer, Jr., following his untimely death. That which I could not put my finger on, that which did not sit well with me, that which seemed to be a hidden agenda, was about to raise its head. A member of New Mount Church had trickled information to the Bishop of the Diocese, "Pastor Agen Depart was holding secret meetings with selected members regarding leaving New Mount

Church." Many of these members secretly meeting with Pastor Depart were members who had united under his Pastorate.

What was rumored became a reality. Five years after becoming the Pastor of New Mount Church, Pastor Agen Depart departed the church with many of the members to start a new independent church. Pastor Agen Depart said his resignation from the church was based on the Bishop, aided by a small group in the congregation, and irreconcilable differences.

Once again through the Spirit of Divine preparedness, the Holy Spirit impressed on me just like five years prior, I would be asked to return to New Mount Church as the interim Pastor. Well, I did get the call, and I did follow God's lead to be reconciled to New Mount Church. Reconciled back to New Mount Church, released of childhood baggage, having an opportunity to grieve, and having an opportunity to be moved in many spiritual ways I just can't explain!

The Shout!

I will never forget the Sunday in Los Angeles, California, where I felt the presence of the Lord so strongly. The Holy Spirit uncorked shouts of joyful praises as I freely lifted up my hands. I am so glad it was not the last of my spiritual experiences.

Bishop Charles Price Jones, the founder of the Church of Christ (Holiness) U.S.A. once said, "I began to seek Him with all my heart for power that would make my life wholly His…I was not satisfied with a faith that brought no fruit, or else fruit so poor a quality spiritually, and a religion that none of the signs spoken of in the scriptures followed."

– Mark 16:14-18; Hebrew 2:1-11

"As we sought God, the Spirit promised that if we fasted three days and nights, He would sanctify us: which we did, and we were filled with light; with joy; and with the Holy Ghost: O, the splendid glory of the exalted state!"

I am so grateful to God allowing what I call, "Freedom Sunday" be a stepping stone for spiritual gifts He bestowed upon me as I earnestly desired. Not for self-gratification, rather to speak more freely to and for God, along with the purpose of edifying others. *– 1 Corinthians 14:1-9*

The Reconciliation Shout!

We all have a past, and not everything in our past has been good for us. There were joyful events, as well as events that brought fear, anger, disgust, and pity to our mental state. It is when these unresolved problems affect our current relationships, interfere with our goals and desires, that we have unfinished business. When I returned to New Mount Church, it was a blessing that Betty Crammer and I were able to work so well together. We both had an opportunity to accept and apologize for our grief reactions following the death of Pastor Ron Crammer. I am so fortunate that we were able to handle our unfinished business. Following a long walk on "The Strand" of Manhattan Beach on December 26, 2003, I returned home to learn from a sobbing church member and my wife that Betty Crammer was suddenly moved beyond her pain. I was honored to eulogize her.

God is so awesome in his approach and involvement in divine intervention towards reconciliation. God impressed on my heart that I could not finalize this book until I tried to make reconciliation with two brothers who I previously viewed as obstacles of conflict, opposed to stepping stones for unity and growth. Recall the Military Chaplin, and Pastor Agen Depart.

It was the death of my mentor Pastor Rod Crammer, Jr. that facilitated the paths of conflict with both of these men. Twelve years later it would be two deaths which would bring about opportunities of reconciliation.

The Reconciliation Shout!

I learned of the death of the Military Chaplain's mother, a faithful missionary. She had impacted many lives in California but died in another state. The decision was made for convenience sake to have the funeral service in that state. I received a phone call from the Military Chaplain, asking if I would consider hosting a memorial service in Los Angeles, California, at New Mount Church, the church where I hold my Pastorate. This would allow local parishioners and friends impacted by his mother to celebrate her life. I happily obliged and assisted with the promotion of the memorial service.

On August 28, 2005, the memorial service was held as God's divine intervention for reconciliation continued to take shape. How?

On Labor Day, September 5, 2005, I received a phone call from the former Military Chaplain stating that he had left his portable CD player holder at the Church. He asked if he could retrieve his belongings on his way to LAX airport prior to his flying to Germany and then on to South Africa.

For me this would not be the usual Labor Day Holiday where we pause to honor workers; rather it would be the Labor Day that I would be working to share my heart with my guarded friend. I told the Chaplain that I would retrieve the CD player holder from the church and meet him at the Magic Johnson Starbuck's coffee shop on Century in Los Angeles for delivery and conversation. I also asked if I could talk with him for awhile, to which he was agreeable, informing me he would arrive in plenty of time prior to his flight's departure.

So there we are sitting in Starbucks drinking our caffeine, exchanging small talk, when I dove into the main matter at hand.

I started with an apology for allowing so many years to drift by without sharing my conflicted feelings towards his actions in 1993.

I started with the "The Robe." I expressed suspicion of the chaplain displaying the robe over my fallen mentor's pulpit seat; this suspicion had galvanized over the years. As I continued to share my conviction, I was totally unarmed when he said, "Yea, I heard about that robe incident and I had nothing to do with it. I learned from my mother how you handled the display. I was so proud of you, I mean knowing you had the testicles (he was more explicit) to remove the robe."

To think all these years I harbored all these bitter feelings toward the Chaplain that were unfounded. As I apologized even more, the chaplain would communicate something even more profound. Accepting my apology, he said,

"It must have been tough for you to wrestle with thinking I was upset with you, because you removed the robe."

The truth of the matter, I had been so convinced and angry that he orchestrated what I viewed as a morbid ritual, I had not even considered what he might be feeling. Talk about pious on my part. Well, since I had egg already on my face, I continued with communicating how upset I was when learning that he departed the Church without mentioning or compensating for long distance calls he made.

I must say that after the bombshell of clarity I received regarding the "Robe saga," whatever explanation the chaplain gave was much less of an issue for me as we sat there drinking our caffeine.

For what it's worth, the chaplain both apologized for and defended his actions communicating, "that Pastor Crammer was known and loved by many throughout the country, and he was merely notifying those individuals about his death and pending funeral." On this day at Starbucks, I was not going to further question the Chaplain's integrity. We caught up on events in our lives and ended with joint prayer.

The death of a church member, Mother (someone older and respected) Manchester Chapel, who died at age 96, birthed the second opportunity for reconciliation. Although she died on August 23, 2005, the Funeral service would not be held until September 1, 2005, to allow her family members to travel from northern California to handle funeral arrangements. I received a phone call from the niece of the deceased, requesting that I officiate and provide the eulogy of the service. Unfortunately, I had to inform her that I could not honor her request, given I had been summoned for jury duty, which I felt I needed to complete since I had requested prior postponements. So who would I ask to take my place in eulogizing this cherished Christian Woman? Immediately I thought of Pastor Agen Depart, but why Pastor Depart and not another pastor with no relationship drama at hand?

He was certainly not one that I had maintained ongoing contact with. From time to time, I would see him at special events such as funerals, concerts, conferences, and even a couple of times bumping into him at a grocery store and pharmacy. The contacts were always polite and causal, but I found these encounters with Pastor Agen Depart hard to engage.

He appeared scurried and guarded, and perhaps he might describe me the same, but each time we met, I felt it was the result of Divine intervention paving the way for relational reconciliation. God placed him on my mind because Mother Manchester was under his pastorate for five years prior to my returning to New Mount Church, yet God was doing something greater as He continued to set the stage for relationship harmony.

I contacted the niece of Mother Manchester, informing her of my dilemma along with my recommendation of Pastor Agen Depart officiating the service, pending his availability.

I obtained the phone number to Pastor Agen Depart's church, using directory assistance. I dialed the phone number and a former member of New Mount Church answered. This former member was happy to hear my voice, and I was happy to hear his voice, but it was also a reminder of the reality of the ugly church split seven years prior. He listened to my need to speak with Pastor Depart. Although Pastor Depart was not in the office at the time, he agreed to pass on the message to him. I soon received a call back from Pastor Depart, and after a period of exchanging niceties, he expressed honor in being able to officiate and provide the eulogy for the funeral service of Mother Manchester Chapel. The service would be held at a local mortuary, the choice of the family. Members from New Mount Church would attend this service along with former members who journeyed with Pastor Depart. Too bad I would not be able to attend, so I thought. On the day prior to the funeral service I was excused from jury services, "How dare they excuse me after my being so willing to serve this time around!"

I would call my wife who works for the Superior Courts, "Honey, they kicked me off the case." She said, "Now honey don't take it personal; just know that you've fulfilled your civic duty."

I continued to see the handwriting on the wall of God's divine intervention. He allowed me to be released from jury duty in order that I would be able to attend the funeral service of Mother Manchester Chapel. There was no thought of asking Pastor Agen Depart to relinquish giving the eulogy after having asked him. He seemed so surprised to see me walk into the service, "Pastor Robert, is that you?" After being invited to join him on the rostrum, he expressed to me that he would not have any problem handing back over to me the eulogy spot. I reassured him that it would be best for him to continue as planned, and I would give brief remarks. As I sat there taking in the moment, made possible by the death of a godly mother, I was sitting in the environment of a united membership that had been broken because of conflict. I was sitting behind and listening to a wonderful eulogy from a member of the clergy who had caused so much apprehension for me in the past. After the interment, I communicated with

Pastor Depart that I wanted to meet with him for breakfast in the near future to share my heart with him. The invitation was warmly accepted.

That breakfast invitation became a reality a month later at the Coffee Company Restaurant in Westchester, California.

I arrived at the crowded restaurant at 10 a.m., a few minutes early of our agreed upon time. Bringing my first cup of coffee to my lips, I pondered what a difference thirteen years made.

I was about to have breakfast with the former Pastor of New Mount church. Yes, the very man whom I held so much indifference to following the circumstances and process of his election to the Pastorate.

I sat at the table anticipating my conversation with this man of God, whom I held in contempt in my heart because he ignored my congratulatory letter and offer of transitional assistance.

The waiter returned to warm my cup with fresh hot coffee. I expected Pastor Depart's late arrival given traffic and this being his first time to the restaurant. This was enough time to reflect on the circumstances surrounding his departure from New Mount Church following his five years' stay, that by his evaluation he deemed, "irreconcilable differences." Just as I was about to take another sip of my coffee, in walks Pastor Agen Depart. We exchanged pleasant greetings and ordered our breakfast meals. I thanked him for making himself available.

I began to share why I was so pleased to meet for breakfast when he politely interrupted me and said, "Robert before you go on, I want you to know how much I appreciate your opening up your life (he had heard about my molestation); you have helped me a great deal." The remarks from Pastor Depart placed me much more at ease given what I would be sharing with him.

I commenced sharing with him about my book writing

venture, and that I could not close the book without having God-prompted reconciliation with him. I continued by apologizing for harboring ill feelings toward him following the death of my mentor.

In addition, I shared it was unacceptable for me to wait so long to start the reconciliation process.

I shared with him that I did not totally understand why God permitted the order of events to unfold as they did, but the sum total of the events manifested incredible freedom for me.

I expressed my feelings about him, not acknowledging my congratulatory letter and offer to assist him in understanding the church dynamics.

Pastor Agen related, "Robert, I vaguely remember getting the letter, and knowing the Agen Depart back then, I most likely did not read the letter; knowing the Agen Depart back then, I probably viewed it just as something customary." He paused, and said in such a genuine manner, "Robert I want to really apologize for that." There was something else that stood out in his acknowledgement and demeanor. For him to say, "the Agen Depart back then," meant that I was dealing with a different Agen today. I could really relate to the statement because he was conversing with a different Robert today.

I was surprised to hear Pastor Depart communicate his initial hesitancy coming to New Mount Church because of hearing about some of the members and operation of New Mount. I further learned that he was bothered that most of the local Pastors had not expressed happiness at his arrival; rather they exercised standoffishness.

My heart was warmed as he voiced having much more appreciation for ministry than he did before. His demeanor and level of conversation made that very obvious and very encouraging to me.

Pastor Agen Depart was very open and invited me to ask of him any questions I had about his departure from New

Mount Church. Questions that I did not need to ask, as he gave me full details how it came about, details which I was already familiar with. It was refreshing to hear his angle of events.

I told Pastor Depart that I did not stand in judgment of his decision, but the circumstances of his coming and leaving New Mount set in motion my freedom!

We spent our remaining time talking about the ministries God has entrusted to us. Pastor Depart was now in his seventh year at the church he founded. What a blessing it was to exchange evangelism desires and programs to broaden.

Yes, it was my regret that we did not have this conversation until thirteen years later, but the good news is that we did have the conversation. We ended our two-and-a-half hour breakfast with prayer and a commitment that we would stay in touch. Oh, the sweetness of relational reconciliation! I looked down at my plate and noticed that I had eaten less than half of my turkey omelet, but I was filled with the fruit of reconciliation.

> *Behold, How good and how pleasant it is for brethren to dwell together in Unity! It is like precious ointment upon the head, that ran down upon the beard, even Aaron's beard: that went down to the skirts of his garments; As the dew of Hermon, and as the dew that descended upon mountains of Zion: for there the Lord commanded the blessings, even life for evermore.*
> *– Psalm 133:1-3*

Thank you Lord for allowing me to see the benefits of mourning as even healing for relationships. I am reminded:

> *A Good name is better than precious ointment; and the day of death than the day of one's birth. It is better to go to the house of mourning, than to go to the house of feasting: for that is the end of all men; and the living will lay it to his heart.*
> *– Ecclesiastes 7:1-3*

Thank You Lord for reminding me of the ministry of reconciliation.

> *Therefore, if anyone is in Christ, he is a new creation; the old has gone, the new has come! All this is from God, who reconciled us to himself through Christ and gave us the ministry of reconciliation: that God was reconciling the world to himself in Christ, not counting men's sins against them. And he has committed to the message of reconciliation. We are therefore Christ's ambassadors, as though God were making his appeal through us. We implore you on Christ's behalf: Be reconciled to God. God made him who had no sin to be sin for us, so that in him we might become the righteousness of God. – 2 Corinthians 5:17-21 (NIV Young Discover's Bible)*

> *Brethren, if a man be overtaken in a fault, ye which are spiritual, restore such an one in the spirit of meekness; considering thyself, lest thou also be tempted. Bear ye one another's burdens, and so fulfill the law of Christ.*
> *– Galatians 6:1-2*

> *Moreover if thy brother shall trespass against thee, go and tell him his fault between thee and him alone: if he shall hear thee, thou hast gained thy brother. – St. Matthew 18:15*

> *These things have I spoken unto you, that my joy might remain in you, that my joy might be full. This is my commandment, that ye love one another, as I have loved you.*
> *– St. John 15:11,12*

"All that waiting is a shout!"

Now all has been heard; here is the conclusion of the matter...

> *Those who sow tears shall reap joy. Yes, they go out weeping, crying seed for sowing and return singing, carrying their sheaves.*
> *– Ps. 126:5-6 (LB)*

The Reconciliation Shout!

I shout because Jesus took up my infirmities, carried my sorrows, shielded me from critical injuries, rejuvenating my life for His glory.

I shout because I am on the other side of circumstances, I have found the fruit of healthy relationships established by God before the foundation of the world; He has allowed me to be holy and without blame before Him in love.

I shout because God has given me the ability to forgive…even the perpetrator of my molestation. No weapon of shame or demonic stronghold formed against me has prevailed, and God has countered my dark history, with a life of light.

I shout because I am made in God's Image. Despite wrong choices I have made in life, I have learned obedience, no longer feeling wounded, scared and dejected, but empowered.

I shout because God has blessed me with the union of marriage, and because marriage is honorable in the sight of God. I feel so blessed to say the union between me and my beloved is holy as we continue to renew our love and commitment before God into eternity.

I shout because of the detours of my life, which became blessed as they allowed for safe destination arrival. Greater learning lies ahead from God, the Master teacher.

I shout because of life's lessons, and the beauty and importance of time shared with my sons. I'm slowing down to marvel over their growth and development into manhood. Blessed am I to live a life of faith that they may model.

I shout because Christ in his death so beautifully provided an example of removing a barrier, that allows people back into the right relationship with God. Before I closed my eyes God allowed me to restore relationships with two men of God, bringing together union of peace following 13 years of discord.

I shout because my calling has been without repentance and God has made room for my gift, as I returned back to

New Mount Church pregnant with anticipation of God's mission and vision to be fulfilled.

I shout because ongoing spiritual liberation directed by the Holy Spirit, anointing me afresh, with ability, qualification, strength, and responsibility to be a blessing to others. No longer anxious, but prayer driven, thankful, transformed.

> ...*Fear God and keep his commandments, for this is the whole duty of man. For God will bring every deed into judgment, including every hidden things, whatever it is good or evil.* – Ecclesiastes 12:13-14

Yes, triumphant consequences have resulted from the cry of my youth to the *shout* of my *journey*.

Shout With Me, *hallelujah (praise God)!*

> *So I went down to the potter's house, and I saw him working at the wheel. But the pot he was shaping from the clay was marred in his hands; so the potter formed into another pot, shaping it as it seemed best to him.* – Jer. 18:3-4

> *Call unto me and I will answer thee and show thee great and mighty things which thou knowest not.* – Jer. 33:3

> *Blessed be the God and Father of our Lord Jesus Christ, who hath blessed us with all spiritual blessings in heavenly places in Christ.* – Ephesians 1:3

> *Be still before the Lord and wait patiently for him; do not fret when men succeed in their ways, when they carry out their wicked schemes. Refrain from anger and turn from wrath; do not fret-it leads to only evil.* – Ps. 37:7-8 (NIV)

> *You can be very sure that the evil man will not go unpunished forever. And you can also be very sure that God will rescue the children of the godly.* – Prov. 11:21 (LB)

> *...No eye has seen, no ear has heard, no mind has conceived what God has prepared for those who love him.* – 1 Cor. 2:9 (NIV)

When I was a child, I thought like a child, I reasoned like a child. When I became a man, I put childish ways behind me. — 1 Cor. 13:11 (NIV)

There is a way that seems right to a man but in the end leads to death. — Prov. 14:12 (NIV)

If the Lord delights in a man's way, he makes his steps firm; though he stumble, he wil not fall, for the Lord upholds him with his hand. — Ps. 37:23-24

No weapon forged against you will prevail, and you will refute every tongue that accuse you. — Isaiah 54:17

For this reason a man will leave his father and mother and be united to his wife, and the two shall become one flesh. This is a profound mystery-but I am talking about Christ and the Church. However, each one of you must love his wife as he loves himself, and the wife must respect her husband.
— Ephesians 5:31-33 (NIV)

Marriage should be honored by all... — Hebrew 13:4

Commit your way to the Lord; Trust in him and he will do this: He will make your righteousness shine like the dawn, the justice of your cause like the noonday sun. — Ps. 37:5-6 (NIV)

...But as for me and my house, we will serve the Lord. — Josh. 24:15

Teach a child to choose the right path and when he is older he will remain upon it. — Prov. 22:6 (LB)

Reverence for God gives a man deep strength; his children have a place of refuge and security. — Prov. 14:26

Therefore, since we have been justified through faith, we have peace with God through our Lord Jesus Christ. — Rom 5:1 (NIV)

For if, when we were God's enemies, we were reconciled to him through the death of His son, how much more, having been reconciled to him through His life! – Rom. 5:10 (NIV)

But the loving kindness of the Lord is from everlasting to everlasting, to those who reverence him; his salvation is to children's children of those who are faithful to his covenant and remember to obey him. – Ps. 103:17 (LB)

Since the Lord is directing our steps, why try to understand everything that happens along the way? – Prov. 20:24 (LB)

Trust in the Lord and do good; dwell in the land and enjoy safe pasture. Delight yourself in the Lord and he will give you the desires of your heart. – Ps. 37:3-4 (NIV)

For the Lord is a sun and a shield: the Lord will give grace and glory: no good thing will he withhold from them that walk uprightly. – Ps. 84:11

And the things you have heard me say in the presence of many witnesses entrust to reliable men who will be qualified to teach others. – 2 Tim. 2:2 (NIV)

Do not be anxious about anything, but in everything, by prayer and petition, with thanksgiving, present your request to God. And the peace of God, which transcends all understanding, will guard your hearts and your minds in Christ Jesus. Finally brothers, whatever is true, whatever is noble, whatever is right, whatever is pure, whatever is lovely, whatever is admirable-if anything is excellent or praiseworthy-think about such things. Whatever you have learned or received or heard from me, or seen in me-put it into practice. And the God of peace will be with you. – Phil. 4:6-9 (NIV)

The Reconciliation Shout!

I am so grateful that God blessed me with my wife Coco, an incredible inspiration to me. I sum up with how she sums me up:

Robert

REDEEMED
OBEDIENT
BEAUTIFUL
ENERGETIC
RECEPTIVE
TOLERANT

Robert has endured much hardship, sickness, and pain.

God's strong arms reached out and caught him, comforted, and called him by name.

God saved him and strengthened his frame; he is no longer the same.

Now you can surely see that he has the victory.

From A Cry to a Shout, the Lord brought him out.

He is no longer a victim but a victor, a mighty man of valor.

From A Cry To a Shout, Robert's life has been transformed; he survived the storms.

From A Cry To A Shout, Robert found out what life is about.

So appreciate and celebrate with a Shout…Let's utter it from our mouth!

From A Cry To A Shout…Praise God without a doubt,
From A Cry To A Shout.

Chapter Notes

1. Rape, Abuse & Incest National Network RAINN 2005 Info@rainn.org.

2. Christian Research Journal Darkening our minds, Vol. 27/No 3, 2004, p. 4.

3. Bishop Emery Lindsay, "Embracing the vision to receive the victory," Church of Christ (Holiness) U.S.A. National Convention, August 1984.

4. Charles P. Jones, "There's a Happy Time A-Coming" His fullness songs, National Publishing Board of Church of Christ (Holiness) U.S.A. 1977.

5. Kristina Sauerwein, "The Friend Trend" Los Angeles Times, 31 August, 1994, p. 3 E1-E5.

6. The Church of Christ (Holiness) U.S.A. Manual of the History, Doctrine, Government, and Ritual, Jackson Mississippi, 1996, p.3.

About the Author

Pastor Robert Hendricks began his high school education at Long Beach Polytechnic High School. His high school experience proved to be a highlight in his life in relation to spiritual and interracial interactions (so proud to be a "Rabbit!").

He graduated from Long Beach Poly High with honors and scholarships in 1976.

Pastor Robert continued his education and earned a B.S. in Social Work at California State University, Long Beach, 1983.

Prior to graduating from college, he met the love of his life and wife of 24 years. They married August 1, 1981. Coco (short for Colleen) and Pastor Robert are the proud parents of Adam and Tyler.

He is the Senior Pastor of New Testament Church of Christ (Hol.) U.S.A., located at 1941 W. Florence Avenue, Los Angeles, California 90047.

Prior to Pastor Robert becoming a full time Pastor, he worked at Long Beach Memorial Medical Center, as a Medical

Social Worker in the Home Health Department for 13 years, and remains affiliated with the Medical Center, serving as a Hospice Chaplain.

Pastor Robert is the President of the Southern Minister's Union and a Member of the Western Diocese Board of Investigation of the Church of Christ (Holiness) U.S.A.

To contact the author for workshops, seminars, speaking engagements or to purchase this book, please call or write:

Pastor Robert Hendricks
New Testament Church
1941 W. Florence Avenue
Los Angeles, California 90047
(323) 750-2211
Email: www.newtestamentchurchla.org

WA

www.ingramcontent.com/pod-product-compliance
Lightning Source LLC
LaVergne TN
LVHW051607070426
83350７LV00021B/2815